EXPANDING FRONTIERS

ABOUT THE AUTHOR

The Rev. Dewi Morgan has been for the last six years on the staff of the Society for the Propagation of the Gospel in Foreign Parts as its Press and Editorial Secretary.

His contributions to *The Church Illustrated* and other Journals have made him well known to many readers.

EXPANDING FRONTIERS

DEWI MORGAN

with a foreword by
CANON MAX WARREN

EDINBURGH HOUSE PRESS
2 EATON GATE, LONDON, S.W.1

First published 1957

Printed by Wm. Carling & Co. Ltd., London & Hitchin

CONTENTS

AUTHOR'S NOTE

It is of the essence of the missionary task that there can be no final statement. But the very newness of the forms in which problems present themselves to each succeeding generation makes imperative a constant assessment, if only to stimulate the questionings which are the sign of watchfulness. This book has regarded its function as being a goad to such questionings. If it leaves the reader insistent on seeking further and more authoritative works it has accomplished its purpose.

I gladly acknowledge my indebtedness to Bishop Stephen Neill's THE UNFINISHED TASK to which these diffuse and inevitably hurriedly written pages owe both their stimulus and their commissioning. Those who are left unsatisfied by the shifting shadows in these covers should go to the substance provided by Bishop Neill.

It need hardly be said that much has happened between the time when this book was written and when it is read. Events, notably in the Middle East and Eastern Europe, have moved rapidly. They have not falsified our principles. They certainly have not diminished our responsibilities.

DEWI MORGAN.

FOREWORD

"Something lost behind the ranges. Lost and waiting for you—Go!" So in Kipling's poem the voice "as bad as conscience rang interminable changes" until the explorer had to leave his border station where the trails ran out and stopped and go on into the 'never never.' Just as that poem superbly reminds us of the moving frontier which has always challenged the enterprise and courage of mankind, so in the book "Expanding Frontiers" Mr. Dewi Morgan has shown us something of what is called for from us as Christians as we too stand on so many frontiers, thinking perhaps that we've reached the end of the journey only to discover that 'the horizon is always further on.'

"There's no sense in going further—it's the edge
    of cultivation."
So they said and I believed it—broke my land
    and sowed my crop—
Built my barns and strung my fences in the little
    border station
Tucked away below the foothills where the trails
    run out and stop.

So said Kipling. But we cannot stop there any more than could the explorer. They are wrong who say "There's no sense in going further." The Christian Church always has to go "on to the bounds of the waste, on to the City of God."

Mr. Morgan in most refreshing style presents us with one after another of the frontiers we have to follow and to cross—"Anything which creates a division between men or divides men from God is against God's will and is a frontier the Christian is called upon to cross. That is the missionary task and it is still unfinished." So Mr. Morgan introduces us to the frontier of the mind of every child born into this world; to the frontiers of race which separate even those united in a common need; to the frontiers of religious experience so variously defined in the religious groupings of mankind; to the frontiers where the technical civilization of the West meets the ancient civilizations of the East; where industrialism and the rural slum compete for the degradation of man. All this and more comes before us in the compass of this small book. It challenges us to further study and to deeper understanding, but it never leaves us oppressed with any sense of hopelessness. We are left with the assurance that He who said "Go" does not leave His obedient servants to advance unaccompanied. And as they advance they know with complete certainty that round one of the bends ahead, perhaps round the next one, they will meet One coming towards them—"Even so, come Lord Jesus."

M. A. C. WARREN.

CHAPTER 1

With the help of my God I shall leap over the wall

IT seems that over 130 manufacturers have found it worthwhile to enter into negotiations with Mr. Walt Disney for the right to add to their products the magic words "Davy Crockett." Judging by the number of small boys (not to mention their elders) who adorn themselves with coonskin caps and pseudo-buckskin jackets, the manufacturers are on to a good thing. Davy Crockett, born 1786, died 1836, is alleged to have sullied his romantic virtues by wife-beating and whisky-swilling, but a public trained to forget unpalatable facts has accepted him as a hero.

The cynic would suggest that Davy Crockett might still be mouldering in a nameless limbo had not astute publicity agents decided to give him immortality. It is perfectly true that vast sums have been spent in creating this present fame. Mr. Disney's pictures demanded that, as did the manufacturers who are prepared to pay up to a shilling in the pound royalty for the use of the name. Publicity has certainly done its work. But the fact remains that Davy offered a suitable subject. And surely its suitability is basically to be found in the fact that he was "king of the wild frontier." His alleged motto, "Be sure you're right and then go ahead" adds to his stature. He may have done sterling work as an American Congressman. He may have been an incredibly good horseman or an incredibly straight shooter. Granted such a variety of prowess his greatness (and who would dare question the appropriateness of the word?) comes from his connection with the frontier.

For frontiers have always fascinated humanity.

Frontiers mark the edge of the known and the beginning of the unknown. Inside our frontiers we are safe and can take life easily. The familiar slippers are cosy beside the familiar fireplace. Outside there are all the hazards. There is, however, something deep in each human which makes life unsatisfying if we always wear bedroom slippers. Cosiness is not enough for a full grown man. The whole history of human development has been that of pioneers crossing new frontiers and looking longingly at the frontiers beyond. Today, sated as we are with all things material and with the feeling that earth's farthest corner has become part of our own backyard—or at least, part of our own sitting room where it appears regularly on the TV screen—we have found yet further frontiers to peer over. Space fiction is among today's most profitable categories for an author, for imaginary tours at supersonic speeds through the outer twilight of remote planets have become the symbol of the Davy Crockett in each one of us.

But space fiction is something which the rational man keeps for his leisure hours. In his fuller life he is able to find frontiers in every part of existence which yet remain unconquered. There is the frontier of art. Can it be said that those who occupy today's *ateliers* have finally succeeded in conveying to those who see their works the communication of their own experience and ideals? In literature, in music, in any of the pursuits where creative spirit must be wedded to technical proficiency, there are still frontiers to be crossed and new and perhaps more glorious territories to be opened up.

So, too, in the world of the mind. Would it not be true to say that the more that is learnt of the mind, the conscious and the subconscious, the more the student acknowledges the mysteries of our inner depths? There are many gaps to be bridged before our knowledge is complete.

And is it not legitimate to regard each new baby born into this world as presenting a new frontier which the rest of the world must somehow cross if that child and its neighbours are to be in any sense common and united members in society? The individuality to which our western ways of thought gives such unqualified lip-service must be integrated with a million other individualities.

All these are frontiers. But recognising them must not be allowed to obscure the fact that even in a world shrunk by science, geographical frontiers still remain. Such frontiers are perhaps more embattled with defence strongpoints than they have ever been. Try getting a visa for a place like Czechoslovakia if you don't believe it.

Frontiers fascinate humanity because they offer a challenge. Why then is it that Christians, to whom above all such a challenge should be a tocsin, sometimes gaze hopelessly at the customs barriers and the barbed wire entanglements which bedevil such frontiers or even, lost in their dim religious light, fail to see such things at all? Any convinced Christian must at once be fully aware of the frontiers of this world and of the fact that it is only in Christ Jesus that they can be removed.

This book is concerned to ask just what are our modern frontiers and what are the representatives of Christ doing in 1957 to surmount them. We want to know what divides man from God and man from man.

The first glance at the needs of the twentieth century world on the one hand and the efforts made by Christians to meet them on the other reveals such a disparity that a further question thrusts itself upon our attention. If

Christians are, comparatively speaking, doing so little, can it be because it is not really their job? Are Christians called out of this world? Can they best fulfil their calling by adjuring this world and finding refuge in some insulated and isolated sanctuary? There are few people in any sort of pew who would subscribe to such a theory in words. Equally there are few church committees or councils which would admit to it in their minutes. But mere words unaccompanied by actions are worse than stillborn. "Not everyone that *saith* unto me, Lord, Lord . . ." is a solemn warning.

What, then, is expected of us?

Roughly speaking, Christians can be divided into those who put more emphasis on the Bible as their authority and those who put more emphasis on the Church. Neither provides any escape from the missionary commitment— which is quite inevitable for both Bible and Church centre around our Lord and the very fact of the Incarnation is basically a *missionary* act initiated by God himself. "God so loved that he *sent*. . . ."

Perhaps the most astonishing thing is the awareness of the earliest chapters of the Bible of this missionary duty. A peasant nation, for most of its history quite insignificant, despised by its neighbours and often in some conqueror's chains, became the midwife of God's greatest act of love. Right from the beginning of its history this nation, wayward as it was, self-centred as were its activities, knew in some subconscious way that God is the Father of all men, though both their words and their actions often denied it. The whole missionary story of the Church lies, in germ, in the first chapter of Genesis. When God divided the waters above the firmament from the waters below he did not limit himself to those waters which lap the shores of Palestine. When he created every living creature he gave

14

them his whole world to live in, "Fill the waters of the seas and multiply on the earth," were the keynotes of the Creation story. But the Genesis account does not linger long over the creation of the animal and vegetable worlds. All that was "formed" by God. Then came the next step when he made man "in his image" and "breathed" in his nostrils. There is a clear distinction between "forming" and "breathing." It is this distinction which is at the heart of the missionary task. God not merely created man. He created man-in-relationship to himself. God brings into existence a world for which he may care. He makes man unto his own image so that he may enter into communion with him. The whole of the Bible, as is the whole art of living, is concerned with relationships—is concerned with transcending frontiers, a fact which finds its ultimate expression in the vision in which "there is neither Jew nor Greek, there is neither bond nor free, neither male nor female; for ye are all one in Jesus Christ." Here the frontiers go toppling. Accidents of race, of social status, even God's own ordained accident of sex, are all obliterated in the final realisation of man-in-relationship with God, the indissoluble link between Creator and creature, between Father and child.

The first chapter of Genesis makes it clear the initiative lies with God. The rest of the Bible develops that statement.

It is in that same first chapter that we learn that God is sole and God is sovereign. It is true that the Jews themselves took a long time to learn that there is but one God. But is it not the case that God reveals far more than those who first get the vision are able to understand and interpret? The mysteries which God reveals today through some humble witness in an Indian village are probably quite beyond the full apprehension of many of the

15

villagers. But that does not diminish their truth, or lessen the duty of bearing witness.

And God is sovereign. God has that sovereignty which so startlingly gives its strength into captivity and seemingly allows the kingdoms of this world to assert and sustain their arrogant claims.

It was as the prophets thundered forth their message that the people of the Old Testament learnt that this sole, sovereign and all-initiating God was also a moral God, making ethical judgments, consumed by ideals of goodness and forever motivated by love. Perhaps it was this realisation which was the greatest step towards distinguishing the Israelites' God from the gods of their neighbours. Quite certainly it is this realisation which distinguishes the Christian idea of God from the theologies of other religions today. And because the idea of God is different, so too is the idea of man different.

Because the God of the Bible has made man "in his image," then in some way man must share in God's attributes, though these he can never possess in his own right but always and only as the gifts of God. It was because of their idea of the spiritual endowments of man that the Israelites came to learn of the Covenant, the root of their religion. In this Covenant they accepted a God who had first chosen them. The Covenant was finally and utterly binding, even if it were broken. It depends upon the righteousness of God and that means that if man does not fulfil his part of it then God, being still faithful to it, must punish. But however God may punish he can never finally abandon. It is this which is the basis of all the Old Testament optimism and foundation of the knowledge of the Messiah. It was because of their view of God and man that they were always forward-looking. The golden age belongs to the future. Judaism, like Christianity, is an expectant religion. But before God's plan can finally be fulfilled man must somehow be brought back into the right relation and must be made fit for that relationship. Like the act of creation, this, too, can be the act of God alone. But such an act cannot be limited to one kind of people or to any single nation. In theological terms, the whole process of redemption must have a universal validity. In more human language, God's family cannot be complete until all the children know and love the Father and act in harmony with his will. Which means that no man enjoys the full relationship with God until all men do.

That being the case, one might legitimately ask why God chose to reveal himself through such an unpromising channel as these Middle East rustics. Would he not have made his message more rapidly and more universally known by choosing some other action? As W. N. Ewer has commented:

> How odd
> Of God
> To choose
> The Jews.

If there is any reason for this choice it may have no small bearing upon our own commitments as twentieth century bearers of the message.

It is not enough to say that Israel had a "genius" for religion and therefore God chose it as his vehicle. Nor is it really satisfactory to say that it was because God chose Israel as his vehicle that Israel was given its genius for religion.

The first point to be made is that had God's revelation been diffuse, had it been equally spread over many nations, then its meaning might well have been lost to humanity. It would not be until the nations had achieved

sufficient unity among themselves that they could fit together the pattern of their cultures and their information
and build up a complete picture of God's providence.
Furthermore, the only conceivable preparation for God
becoming Man in one place at one time was that one
nation should go through a long period of preparation to
make ready the human context in which the Incarnation
would happen.

While we can never presume to claim fully to know
God's reasons and reasonings, it would seem that the para-
doxical quality which marked out the Hebrew nation for
this unique honour of being God's chosen instrument was
its insignificance and weakness. This very choice offers a
good illustration of God's unconditional initiative. He does
not choose Israel because she is in any way better than
her neighbours. She has no particular righteousness, no
particular virtue. God's vocation is not dependent on a
man's worth.

The Hebrews were for ever at the mercy of their more
powerful neighbours. Had Israel been more powerful she
would have needed no salvation from Egypt that she could
not obtain for herself. It was in that very act of being
released from bondage that so much of God's nature was
revealed. It was because Israel was in deep need that she
had the capacity of serving God's purpose. God's choice
of Israel was a statement not about Israel but about himself.

It was because Israel was at the mercy of her powerful
neighbours that she found a unity other than the material.
It was because Israel was weak that she experienced all
the hard lessons of Babylon and lost her last lingering
respect for the old nature gods. Divorced from the Temple
she learnt that mercy is more important than sacrifice. It
was the Exile which made them a People as it was the

Exile which caused their influence to flow beyond their own boundaries.

It was in the Exile that Israel began to discover that passivity can be activity, that sometimes you can do most by letting things be done to you.

The whole history of Israel is a long training and discipline in those qualities which were to become finally manifest in the Suffering Servant.

The Old Testament is the record of such a development. That, in itself, is enough to make it an outstanding missionary book, throwing so much light on what is expected of us. But even more important, the Old Testament was the Book which became the beloved text of God made man when in the fulness of time he came. It was the Book Jesus used. It was about the contents of this Book that he said "I am come not to destroy but to fulfil." And it was this same Book which was the school-master of his disciples who, being Jews, yet took their faith beyond their own nation and were the first to show that it was indeed a light to lighten the Gentiles.

So much for the Old Testament. But when we come to the New Testament the expression of our commitment becomes at once so vast and so obvious—to him who will look—that we can but touch the surface in this book. It was Edward Shillito who reminded us of G. K. Chesterton sitting on the South Downs and wishing he had a piece of chalk with which he could draw. Chesterton, of course, remembered that the whole hill on which he sat was made of chalk. So, too, says Shillito, the whole of the New Testament is a missionary Book. We can only glance at some of its points.

In his cradle Jesus was visited by Magi from distant lands, his Cross was carried by someone traditionally from Africa. It was a Samaritan, not a Jew, who earned the adjective "Good" and it was a Gentile soldier whose faith was commended above that of the Jews. Jesus found Nineveh and Tyre in less danger of retribution than his own Jerusalem. And the whole picture given in the Gospels is of a flawless exhibition of the possibilities of human sonship based on the recognition of the divine Fatherhood. Such a conception of God and man becomes quite meaningless if it is to be limited by any human accident of race or colour. Any frontiers which are allowed to remain are a denial of the overflowing divine love which leaps across all frontiers.

The effect of this new idea of God and man upon those who had the grace to see it is the subject of the *Acts of the Apostles*. St. Luke seems deliberately to have chosen his material to illustrate the greatest possible breadth. In this ever-widening account we see the progress of the expansion of Christianity from Jerusalem to Rome. The new Faith comes into contact with one culture after another. It breaks into new social surroundings. In all of them it shows it has the same meaning and the same effect. But St. Luke is concerned in the Acts with something much greater than mere reportage—essential as such is to a truly historic religion. St. Luke is concerned with giving us an insight into the Christian motive—to be *apostles,* to be men who are sent.. His story tells of men who, convinced that Jesus is in the fullest sense still alive, break through all frontiers in the power of his Spirit.

The broad canvas of the *Acts of the Apostles* is supplemented by the Epistles. And what need to labour the fact that St. Paul was a missionary? Every letter bubbles with the urgency of a missionary who worried over his converts like a faithful sheepdog over his master's sheep. What is perhaps more necessary to point out is that the difficulties which St. Paul faced are so much the difficulties which missionaries in 1957 face in so many parts of the world. How was the Christian to react to heathen vices and social habits? What was to be the relationship between Church and State? What was the Church to do about a convert who wanted to retain vestiges of his old religion? How does the Christian idea of God differ from the pagan's? St. Paul grappled with those questions and so does the twentieth century missionary.

The Bible ends as it begins. The writer of *Revelations* is offering encouragement to a church under persecution. Christians undergoing suffering are bidden to remember they are in the hands of the Lord of history and that history will culminate in a heavenly kingdom which will be "out of every nation." "They shall bring the glory and honour of the nations into it."

Throughout the Bible there is the clear recognition that there are frontiers. There are frontiers between nation and nation, between rich and poor, between wise and unwise, between "the Kingdom" and "the world." The Bible does not minimise these frontiers but it does very clearly tell us that under God and in his Son and through the power of his Spirit we are charged to go on surmounting them until in the final moment of God's love they are no more. Anything which creates a division between men or divides men from God is against God's will and is a frontier the Christian is called upon to cross. That is the missionary task and it is still unfinished.

Chapter 2

"That there be no divisions among you"

"Two thousand years ago there lived a Man. In a small unimportant country, he lived his simple life, never in contact with the world leaders of his day, almost unnoticed by the historians of his time. What can he have to do with us in our driving, twentieth century, mechanised world of today, in our high-pressure offices, at our noisy, ostentatious cocktail parties, in the stress and worry of trying against rising costs to make a living or support a family? That Man —Christ Jesus—manifested with convincing force, as nobody else in history has ever been able to do, what God, the great God who made the world, is like. He revealed God, the all-powerful, as a Being of supreme love—all gentleness, as understanding as a human father. Prophetic souls before him had coupled God with supreme power but never with supreme tenderness and love, as Christ did. Profound insight—or audacious folly! This revolutionary conception has upset kingdoms and changed the course of empires. It has generated more irresistible power than any other force in history. Great armies, incomparable arrays of material strength, have not been able to withstand it. Today, twenty centuries after his death, his unforgettable words still ring across the world with resurgent, revitalising power."

Francis B. Sayre.

OF course you have heard all that before. Perhaps therein lies the tragedy because familiarity breeds indifference, if not contempt. But try to see those words afresh and ask yourself how such things can possibly be. The answer lies outside the purely human categories. And yet the answer is infinitely simple. The Christ who came to earth two thousand years ago is the source of power today because he died and rose again and resumed his glory. More than that even, he promised his strengthening Spirit and for the fulfilment of that promise, collected a band of men—ordinary men, through whom that Spirit would work. The works that Jesus did on earth were to be extended all through time through the Spirit and his household, the Church.

The Incarnation was the prime missionary act. God *sent.* . . . The Church therefore inevitably partakes of that missionary character. To talk of "the missionary work of the Church," if it implies that work is in any sense an optional extra, is to betray a lamentable ignorance. The Church *is* missionary. It is a *sent* Church and any single member who forgets that he too is sent forfeits the fulness of membership. The Church can never linger at the base camp, never sojourn in the fastnesses of fortified strongholds. Its place is at the frontiers. And as those frontiers expand, so too the Church is *sent* ever further and further.

With the inspired directness of his greatness, William Temple had a word for it. "The Church exists for those who are not yet its members." Should it be deduced from that statement that the Church will no longer exist when all men are its members? Can it be said that the missionary Church is suicidal in that in the moment of its final success it automatically dissolves itself as no longer necessary?

Perhaps that is the sort of question which should be

merely voiced in this book while we use up such space as we have on less academic issues. For the thought contained in our title is that, until the end of the age, the Church cannot have complete success. The frontiers Christianity besieges are ever being pushed back. As fast as we cross one we find another. Life is dynamic and not static. And in a fallen world the energy which makes life dynamic is perverted. Until the time of the harvest there will be both the powers of darkness and the Church as well as the tares and the wheat growing together. We merely delude ourselves if we believe God has promised his Church complete success here and now and the Christian battle is far too serious to allow time for delusions. What God has said is: "I send you forth." Our response is not to be over-confidence or complacency about an early victory. Our response is to be obedient. Not a blind obedience but an obedience aware of the battle with principalities and powers. We are caught up in the process of transmuting the Kingdoms of this world into the Kingdom of God.

But that very suggestion of a complete antithesis between the powers of darkness and the Church makes us pause in our tracks, for it implies that the Church is quite other than and separate from "the world." It is an all too obtrusive fact of experience that the visible Church here on earth sometimes appears infiltrated by the powers of darkness. Only the most naive would venture to distinguish between wheat and tares among those who profess and call themselves Christian or even among those who occupy a pew regularly each Sunday. "Look at the sort of people who go to the local church" is what a pagan often says to excuse his own absence. And sometimes his remarks are unpleasantly near the truth.

Herein lies such a stumbling block that we must either look at it closely now or bark our shins later.

24

There never has been a time in history or a place on the face of the earth where one could confidently take an unbeliever and say "Here is the Church, working and worshipping as God intended it." St. Paul had to criticise those professing Christians of his own day who saw no impediment to going to law before unbelievers—could there be a greater travesty of fellowship? The cultured Brahmin is hardly attracted by illiterate outcasts crowding church doors during a mass movement any more than the Korean gentleman is favourably impressed today when he sees a single branch of the universal Church conducting noisy harangues and permitting new factions amongst its own members. There have been so many periods in history over which Christians would willingly draw a curtain. To illustrate this it is necessary to do no more than mention the Crusades—when men were granted indulgences for forays which were the occasions of the most gross self-indulgence. It is probable that the effect of these Crusades was still being felt at the recent Bandung Conference and will long continue to bedevil relationships between the Church and those who remain outside.

The Church on earth is rarely an entirely lovely sight and there are times when it is a heartrending spectacle. Can we really believe that this is the instrument which Christ planned for his use?

In *The Power and the Glory* Graham Greene gives us a picture of a Roman priest who has become an addict to pretty well every sin of the flesh. He is besotted and horrible and no Christian can follow his tragedy without some feeling of nausea. Yet even when he plumbs the lowest depths he remembers his divine commission. Such a remembrance might do little more than increase his fear of retribution. At no time does his knowledge of his commission save him from sin. At no time is he unaware of the sinful character of his sin. Yet at no time does he forget that Christ has called him to a particular work.

The astonishing thing about this whisky-priest is that he is not schizophrenic. He is one man. There is some entirely mysterious conjunction of the human and the divine. God can and does use even so filthy an agent, just as clean water can flow through a pipe which is outwardly foul.

God can and does use his Church with all its imperfections. For that Church is the instrument of his Son. It is, as the household of his Spirit, the extension of that Son's Incarnation. The sufferings which our Lord felt in his human body, the agony of the cross, the spittings and the scourgings, he still feels in the failings of his Church. For the Church is the act of God carried out through the hands of men. Although St. Peter betrayed our Lord there was yet great work reserved for him to do. But, lest we become complacent about the failings of the human element in the Church, let us never forget that St. Peter's acceptance after his betrayal came only after he had wept. It was after that complete acknowledgement of his weakness and his sin that Peter was given the inestimable privilege "Feed my lambs."

The renewal which occurred in the life of Peter has been so marked a characteristic of the history of the Church. There have been times when any merely human observer, however much he wanted otherwise, would have been forced to pronounce it finally dead. There have been times when human indulgence has made it a caricature of corruption and reeking luxury. There have been times when sheer pusillanimity has made it the despised lackey of a secular power. There have been times when powerful enemies have delivered a seeming deathblow. Yet the Church is still here. And perhaps one need look no further than the modern history of Russia to see how ineffective is human persecution of the Church—but let no-one minimise the suffering which can be inflicted on the Church. The Church, whether weakened from within or without, seems to acquire a power of renewal which defies analysis in earthly terms. Yet again there are the admonitory fingers of history to wreck any complacency. The time is not yet when the Church will have recovered from the advancing hordes which burst out of Muslim strongholds and gnawed away so much of the heart of the once Christian world. Here, indeed, was a case where the frontiers were very rapidly contracting. And what lesson does that bear for us in our generation?

We have been dealing in extremes and it is too easy to assure ourselves that we are referring to other people. But unless we are forcibly smitten into ejaculating "Oh God, this means me" we have no right to disport ourselves with academic speculation about the nature of the Church. What are the facts for us who live in Britain?

Within easy walking distance of our homes is a building where people gather fairly regularly, where sermons are preached and sacraments are administered, where people wear their best clothes and rather enjoy a good rousing hymn or two and the flowers are usually very pretty. It's a good place to be connected with because it's respectable. If you are the right type you may even be allowed to perform the highest office—carrying round a little green bag into which people drop their small change.

Is that an exaggeration? Pray God that it is. It is perhaps a picture which is now slightly out of date but more of that later.

What we are concerned about now is that this tiny community in the local church is our representation of the Christ who came to bring fire and sword upon the earth, the Man associated with putting down the mighty from their seats and sending the rich empty away (does that sound like our local church?). This is the Man whose followers turn the world upside down. This is the Man who shall come again with glory to judge both the quick and the dead. This the Man who told us—yes, our local church—to go bursting through all the expanding frontiers and establish the bridgeheads of His kingdom and the colonies of heaven in enemy territory. This is the Man who gave us the whole world as our parish.

Can there be any connection between our local church and him? And if so, can "overseas missions" continue to find their place in the annual balance sheet somewhere below "coke for the boiler" and "providing a new cushion for organist"?

It would be sheer disregard of facts to suggest that the Church in the twentieth century is worse than it has been in the past. In fact, we hope to suggest later that the twentieth century may be one of the Church's brighter periods. But that there are congregations which are living proofs of Marx's assertion about religion being an opiate, who can deny? We are committed to seeking an explanation.

The Church is not set here to be a soporific. It is not intended as a cosy club for like-minded people of goodwill. It is not intended to give a slightly intoxicating moral uplift nor is it a divine help towards being rid of your worries and successful living. It is here as the instrument of God's Holy Spirit.

For what?

It is here to proclaim until the end of the age the good news of man in Christ bought back from his enthralment to evil. It is here to show the Mediator through whom Creator and creature are once again one. It is here to administer the Sacraments by which Christians are strengthened for so superhuman a task. It is here to annihilate frontiers of every sort. It is here to point a way from itself to its Master.

The Church is here to preach to all men at all times by all means. Though it is clear that conversion is the object of preaching, yet nowhere is the Church committed to convert. That is the work of God alone. And perhaps a more frequent reminder of that fact would give us greater courage in tackling the job which is set before us. Human beings are so diligent at getting on with what they have not been asked to do. It's a form of escapism from the duties assigned to them.

It is when we remember that our commitment is to preach that we are saved from all the bother and disappointment of counting heads. Statistics are one of modern man's dazzling playthings and it was a wise instinct which made them frowned upon in the Old Testament.

The moment we accept the fact that our commitment is to preach, then it seems to become possible of attainment —even though the sermon be a poor one. But there are two more statements to be added, one of them terrifying and the other reassuring.

Preaching does not mean merely using words. It means everything which can convey the beliefs of one man to another. In fact, preaching means every single act we commit, every single word we say. And since both our acts and our words are conditioned by our thoughts, it also means the thoughts we think. We are committed in our whole being and with our whole being to an incessant proclamation that God so loved the world that he sent his only beloved Son into the world that through him all men might be saved.

Such a realisation is no less than terrifying and must

send us hastening away from the Hound of Heaven. But alongside it must be put the realisation that it is Christ in us who is the Preacher. When all the duties are added up and all the helps are put alongside them, the balance sheet is an easy one. We simply fall back upon Christ and let ourselves live in Him.

The sending which God began at the Incarnation goes on in us today. It is a sending to all men. I am sent.

It is against that realisation that we begin to look at the frontiers.

Chapter 3

"They brought young children to Him"

HAVE you ever had the privilege of watching closely a young mother bathing her first baby for the first time? You will see her tenderness and her love. But if you have her confidence you will also learn of her great nervousness. This precious bundle seems so fragile. And though bred of her own body the very fact of birth involves a separation between herself and that new wriggling mite which has so many possibilities. Between any parent and child there is a frontier and family life is incomplete until it is crossed.

Every new baby born into the world presents an unevangelised frontier which the Church must cross. To each new generation must be transmitted the Faith once delivered to the saints. It is a never ending process and it makes it quite inevitable that, in this dispensation, the task of the Church remains unfinished. There is always work for Christians to do. Millions of challenges are born each year.

The man who realises the effect of the thousand secular forces which afflict the mind of his adolescent son knows how precarious is the handing on of ideals from one generation to another. And that same man will realise that unless he can hand on those ideals they may well be lost forever. It is a truism to suggest that there can be no physical link between my father and my son except myself. Yet the fact that there can be no human link between the

31

Christians of yesterday and the Christians of tomorrow except the Christians of today is one which frequently escapes our attention.

God has let all the continuing of the Christian Faith upon earth rest upon the shoulders of one generation— our generation, which is the only generation available at this moment. That is not to suggest that if this generation entirely fails to hand on that Faith that God is powerless. But it is to assert with all the strength at our command that our generation has been given a responsibility which is equalled only by its privilege of being fellow-workers with God. We are the only human beings to whom God can look for the continuance of his work in this day and age.

Is that a cheering prospect?

Lest we become frightened by the greatness of our vocation, we should remember that for nearly two thousand years God has been depending on people just like us. There have from time to time been giants in the land, giants who have carried the thread through some threatening crisis or held on against the onslaughts of very powerful foes. But for the most part it is the weak things of the earth who have been chosen as the links in God's chain. The work and the power are God's. We are servants of the Almighty.

Having accepted all the comfort those words can give, we face the fact that there have been periods in history when parts of the Church have, as far as the human eye can see, been obliterated, or at least quite incapacitated. When we listen to today's turbulent news from the Middle East how often do we remember that here was the cradle of the Church, here were the first Christian lands? Yet how puny their Christian membership today. Is not St. Sophia, now a mosque, an ever-present reminder that a glorious Christian church can become the trophy of an anti-Christian force?

32

The tragedy of the enslavement of the ancient Christian Church of, say, Egypt by the enemies of Christ can be re-enacted at any time in any part of the world. There is no reason ever to think that because an area is Christian now it will still be so in fifty years' time.

It is perfectly true that history would suggest that persecution has frequently strengthened the Church, that the blood of the martyrs is the seed of the Church. But woe to those who let their faith in God's ultimate victory—a faith which our Lord himself has underwritten—blind them to the efforts which principalities and all the powers of darkness are making and will continue to make. The road to the Resurrection through Calvary is not strewn with rose-buds all the way. Our Lord promised his faithful followers no easy victory.

Perhaps even more dangerous than open persecution is apathy, boon companion of secularism. It is certainly more widespread. It is the enemy which any British person will tell you constantly confronts him. And this indifference can assume such proportions as to suggest the possibilities of a race of complete unbelievers growing up. Each new generation needs its own converting.

A steelmaker will tell you that the worst thing that can happen in his industry is for a furnace to be allowed to cool off while it still contains metal. Once that metal is cold the furnace is useless until the metal has been dug out —a matter of very considerable effort and cost. It is sometimes cheaper to destroy the furnace than to clean it out. A Christian heart which has grown cold is often a greater challenge than a pagan heart which has never been warmed.

Even in Europe, once proudly bearing the fair name of "Christendom," each generation faces anew the possibility of hearts grown cold. Bishop Stephen Neill tells of a Swiss theologian describing the meaning of Confirmation for some boys. "Now I shall start to wear long trousers. Now I shall be allowed to smoke. And now, like Daddy, I shall be able to stop going to church."

You don't have to go to Switzerland to find such an attitude. It seems that two-thirds of the children born in this country are baptised in the Church of England. Less than half of them are confirmed and only a quarter of those become regular communicants. Statistics from other English Churches indicate that the C. of E. is not the only sufferer.

Those figures would suggest a frontier which is not being crossed. The point with which we are concerned for the moment is that those figures obtain in what is called—and not without reason—a Christian country, a country in which there are nearly two thousand years of Christian tradition, where the schools and hospitals have a Christian foundation, where the law is based on a Christian view of the nature of man, where all the authorities are favourable, or, at least, not unfavourable.

Here in a country where so many things are in its favour the Church finds it hard to transmit its message to the young. What, then, do you think it is like in Africa and India for the tiny Church to pass on its message? In Britain a boy is usually helped in his application for a job by a testimonial from the local minister. In Pakistan a boy may have to conceal his Christian allegiance before he can get a job at all. In Ceylon the fact that a child has been at a Christian school may leave him suspected of a westernised education which, by definition, is hostile to the national interests of an eastern State.

The faiths and philosophies which oppose Christianity in Asia are militant. The Church can recognise them openly for what they are and at least is strengthened by the clear nature of the problem. But these visible difficulties are not the only ones.

Consider for the moment the case of an intelligent lad in one of the tiny Christian communities in India or Africa or Togoland or Borneo—or anywhere in the less developed countries. He does well at the village school. He gets a scholarship to the high school. He gets the chance of a college education. Eventually he goes back to his own village. He finds that his parents have intellectually stood still while he has made such advances. He finds the Christian faith of his father devout but so uninformed. He even finds the family diet primitive after he has tasted some more complicated dish at a city restaurant. He finds himself almost a stranger in his own home village. He goes along to renew his acquaintance with the village catechist (there probably won't be an ordained minister available) and finds that the old man who once seemed a fount of wisdom is just a rustic. In sending that lad to college, has the Church created more frontiers than it has removed? Education is one of our most expensive missionary activities, so that question cannot be sidestepped. It is so important that it must be examined even more closely.

Let us suppose that our lad showed a particular bent for one of the sciences. He would have been taught to read and his horizons would have been immensely broadened. But even more important, if he had been able to specialise in a science, he would have been taught a particular attitude of mind which is the mark of the scientist. Science depends on the material. Science, as science, knows only those things which can be measured and weighed. No truth becomes a scientific fact unless it can be repeated under laboratory conditions every time a scientist wishes.

All those things are the right and proper disciplines of science. But unless the boy has learnt that the disciplines of science are not necessarily applicable to all the other realms of man's thought, unless he has learnt that there are other ways of thinking which are as valid as those of the scientist, unless he has learnt that there are truths which by their very nature are outside the scope of science as science, his scientific training, instead of fulfilling his personality, has left him little more than a calculating machine. He is estranged from his home background. There seems little place in which he can take root in a new background. Has the Church been wrong in enabling him to have a scientific education?

Since science has grown up as the child of the western Christian mind, one has only to ask such a question to see its answer. The Lord of all truth wants his children to share his truth—all his truth. And it is the duty of the Church to pass it on.

What the Church has to be concerned about is raising the level of the whole culture from which that boy came. To suggest anything other than that is to imply that we should all have remained in woad and skins enjoying the few amenities of our cave-dwellings.

How is the Church to set about educating an African boy and still maintain his link with his community? How is the Church to demonstrate the true place of a scientific education in an African kraal?

This book is written in the conviction that the only point at which all frontiers come down is in God. Except in him there must forever remain Jew and Gentile, bond and free, black and white. Any merely human attempt to transcend these divisions is unrealistic and leads to the fiction that such frontiers do not exist. That being the case, we who are God's servants have the task of making God known to every community. Just as our Lord sent forth his messengers for this purpose, so must we.

Somehow we have to encompass the humanly impossible and install a dedicated servant of God in every village, in every city slum, in every place where two or three gather together, throughout the world. But putting men and women in such places is not enough. We have to see that they have been given the opportunities of acquiring the knowledge and training which will fit them to proclaim the Way, the Truth and the Life to all sorts and conditions in their communities. They will not all need to have scientific education—awful thought!—but they will all need to be aware of something of the habits of every sort of thinking, for only thus can every sort of thinking be baptised. They will not have to know all the facts and techniques that the specialist knows but they will need to know his attitude of mind if they are in any sense to identify themselves with him and thus lead him to Christ. This is not a plea that every Christian worker should be a walking encyclopaedia but that he or she should be given the greatest possible opportunity of acquiring breadth of mind. This is something more closely aligned with Christian sympathy than with an electronic brain.

It is trite to say that as yet we have not begun to approach the problem. We all know that—and some of us sorrow over it. What we do not all know, or at least recognise, is the infinite need for training for those we send. The village catechist is unable to answer the spiritual difficulties of his scientifically trained schoolboy not because he doesn't know the answers—by virtue of his faith he may well do so, though in an inchoate and unarticulated way. What the catechist doesn't know is the questions. They have never crossed his mind, for he has never had the chance of understanding the mind of the scientist.

Even in the Church at home we find our elders and betters very ready to answer the questions they think we ought to ask but they appear clueless about some of the questions we *do* ask simply because such questions are outside their purview. When I had just been ordained an old and respected priest said to me, "Well, my boy, I hope you are never going to read any more theology; stick to nothing but novels from now on." That man had some journalistic leanings and so inevitably expressed himself somewhat colourfully. But there was more than a grain of truth in his suggestion that to teach our people we need to know not only our subject but also our people and what is in their minds. That involves reading what they read and seeing what they see. There are many schoolteachers in England today who suggest that they cannot really teach their children unless they have been able to give the whole of the previous evening to watching both commercial and B.B.C. T.V. and thus getting up to date on the contents of the children's minds. To teach adequately you have to know both your subject and your pupil.

If English schoolteachers have such problems how much greater are the difficulties faced by a village catechist when a lad fresh back from strange experiences poses unthought-of queries. Somehow we must help that catechist to a richer heritage of thought and experience.

Right across the world today, for those who can read, there is a plethora of reading matter. The children of this world, ever wise in their generation, have seen to it that sex and sensation get their circulation-winning presentation. And the communist world has not been backward in promoting its viewpoint anywhere. There is much food for thought in the fact that in almost all countries it is the Christian Church which has first reduced a language to writing and produced the earliest literature but subsequently this powerful weapon has become the almost exclusive possession of secular forces because of the lack of adequate Christian literature. Why is it that Christians begin some worthwhile job and then falter before its completion?

The need for Christian literature throughout every country is a matter of the utmost urgency now at this moment. As the great literacy campaigns make their impact—and these again are initially under Christian sponsorship—this need must grow and is assuredly second only in importance to the constant need of more and more Christian agents.

But the printed word is not the only influence. When Sir John Glubb came back to this country he said, "The procedure between States in the past was that one government dealt direct with another. In those days it was not possible for one government (by use of radio) to speak direct to the subjects of another government behind the backs of their own government. That is what is possible now and it seems to me as big a revolution in world relations as the invention of the atom bomb." We need do no more than remember Greek broadcasts to Cyprus to confirm Sir John's point.

In remote corners of the earth people are twiddling little knobs and they do not have to be able to read to absorb some hymn of hate which emerges from a loudspeaker. In so many cases the message which the radio conveys is "Down with the West." And, to our eternal shame, we have let the Faith which began in the Middle East become identified with the "western way of life." We have let the Gospel we are sent to proclaim become cluttered up with our all too human preoccupations. We have made Christianity western instead of making the West Christian, with the result that many who are anti-Western think they must be anti-Christian.

There is another facet to this tragedy of the identification of Christianity with the West. People across the world have come to know Hollywood. Brazil has nearly 2,000 cinemas, Burma has nearly a hundred. Asian peasants and South American peons are assured that razor-slashed gangsters and diaphanously draped pin-ups are typical of western life and assume that "Rock 'n Roll" is the acme of its culture.

The lad who went off to college for his scientific education would hardly have failed to visit a cinema occasionally. And his dear and devoted old catechist would be called upon to explain things he could conjure up only by a most frantic effort of the imagination. The scientific lad already has some grounding in the Christian Faith and might be able to assess accurately the value of the celluloid world. But what about all his countrymen who have never even had the chance of hearing the Gospel?

Here the Church is faced not by one frontier but by many frontiers—many barriers—rolled into one mighty obstacle. The forces which build up these barriers seem to come from all sides at once. Which leads us on to another point.

It has been suggested that since Christian agents are so few it might be worthwhile in terms of strategy to centre them all on one area and, under the grace of God, make that so vigorous a Christian strongpoint that its influence would go out in ever widening circles until the whole world was covered. This, of course, is another form of the suggestion that we should convert our own country before we start on someone else's. Those who make such suggestions forget that St. Paul did not wait for Jerusalem to be a Christian city before he began his forays. But there is an even more cogent point than that in the twentieth century.

There is no part of the world which can be isolated and

40

treated as a central point of mission. It is not enough to concentrate all your forces on an Indian city if the people in that city are being subjected to pagan influences from outside. To ensure that all influences are Christian you must edit most of the films those people see, or first convert Hollywood. And you must correct most of the books they see, or first convert the get-rich-quick publisher and the communist propagandist.

For the Christian there is only one world and, while strategic placing of Christian forces in one particular point is of value, we can never forget the wholeness of the task. While each one of us can only do a certain amount and leave the rest, we must each do our bit in the light of the totality of a world united in its needs and sufferings. The more one looks at the world the more evident it becomes that evil and sin have an astonishing kinship across the world. If you manage to suppress them in one corner they seem to become stronger in another. The sins which tempt sailors in Singapore are the same as those in the Port of London. The vice operators who are driven out of Soho can still run their rackets from Belgium and no doubt have branch offices in Hong Kong and Rio. It is the same jealousy, the same greed, the same selfishness which afflicts all mankind and one would sometimes think that Satan has been far more effective in unifying humanity than have been the forces of good—except that, of course, any unity Satan may attain is temporary and specious, for nothing is more divisive than sin in the long run.

We have wandered away from the baby with whom this chapter started and have almost lost the scientific student with whom it has been largely concerned. What are we to say about them? How is the Church to convey its message over the gulf which separates them?

When clergy begin—as they so very frequently do—to

ask what is wrong with our approach to "youth," why so many Sunday School children fail to grow into adult membership, their conclusions seem to run somewhat as follows: "Sunday Schools are not what they should be because of the homes the children come from. Therefore you have to start with the parents. But before you start with the parents you must start with the newly-weds. Before that you must start with the preparation for marriage. But even prior to that comes the training of young people generally. But you must start the training of young people when they are children and, of course, the proper training of children depends on the training of their parents." It is possible to continue this circular tour until it becomes as profitless as the debate on the number of angels who can stand on the head of a pin. But the fact remains, we can examine the problem of the baby and the young man only against the background of people as a whole. We must gird our loins and try that task of getting a picture of twentieth century humanity. It is only well-girded loins, free of all superfluous drapings, which will enable us to leap across the frontiers which are our challenge. Each generation still remains to be won.

Chapter 4

To fill so great a multitude

"OUR population in Singapore is now about 1,200,000 which is 500,000 more than it was eight years ago. Fifty-six per cent of our population is under the age of twenty-one and we require a new school for four hundred children every week if we are to keep pace with the birth-rate." So a missionary wrote recently.

In one lifetime the population of Jakarta has risen from .26 million to 2.8 million.

The Indian Government faces an expectation of the present population of 375 million reaching 510 million in a generation, even though birth control clinics are officially supported.

The population of Japan—nearly ninety million in a land area just a little bigger than the British Isles of which a mere one-sixth is cultivable—is increasing by at least a million and a half a year, despite the fact that there is practically one abortion for every live birth.

The population of Barbados is 1,300 to the square mile. Thirty years ago the rate of increase of population was 300 a year. Now it is 3,800, even though there again birth control is Government promoted.

The baby with whom the last chapter began is just one of two and a half thousand million people and that number is expected to *double* itself each succeeding century.

2,500,000,000 frontiers which the Gospel has to cross. "Go ye into all the world and preach. . . ." It will take a very long time to fulfil our Lord's accompanying command, "baptising them . . ." if only in terms of physical manhours standing at a baptistry.

The Church is confronted with a problem of numbers which is greater than ever and will pretty certainly be greater still. Yet the Church must rejoice in the factors that have produced these increased numbers and is indeed itself responsible for many of them.

The population of the world is increasing more rapidly than ever because so many of the things which once kept the numbers of people down have now been overcome. There was a time when millions of people died annually through starvation. A frighteningly large number still do. But science has learnt to co-operate more fully with the good earth and the rhythm of the seasons, and more food is available. There was a time when disease decimated peoples with monotonous regularity—it is barely a century since London had its last cholera epidemic. Today not only curative medicine but, even more effective, preventive medicine and general hygiene have taught people not to have cesspools below the floorboards of their living rooms. There was a time when our parents had enormous numbers of children partly because few of them were expected to reach adolescence—though, of course, this was not the only reason! Prenatal care and more widespread knowledge of infant welfare have meant that even with smaller families more children grow up.

The headaches which Britain is at present facing in connection with "the bulge"—the large numbers of babies born immediately after the war—which is now passing through the schools, are enough to alert us to the infinitely greater headaches which less developed countries suffer.

And there was a time when fifty or sixty years was considered a long life. Today a man of fifty insists he is in his prime. The growing preponderance of age to youth at least calls for adjustment in many of our national institutions.

The Church must welcome all these things because they represent a signal respect for human life and the removal of suffering. And, of course, it is the Church which is to such a degree responsible for these things. Just as in our own country it was the Church which started hospitals, the care of the aged and poor, education and other evidences of Christian compassion, so too overseas it was the servants of the healing Saviour who were usually the first to lead people to better health in body and mind as well as soul. The epic story of Medical Missions must, by the grace of God, be one of humanity's finest achievements and one which deserves many books of superlative appreciation. Increased populations are largely the result of the Church's work.

But have we fully seen all the implications of worldwide better health? The Church, more than any worldly authority, must seriously ask: where is it all leading? What does it mean for our inescapable commitment to proclaim to all men?

The trouble is that there seems to be no reliable information bureau on the subject. Statisticians pull out their slide rules and draw impressive graphs about numbers of people. But they cannot tell us how they are to be fed, or clothed, or housed, or employed, or educated to the fullness of their abilities. Nor how they can be evangelised. Scientists are constantly engaged in a lively battle among themselves about the maximum world potentialities in world food production. They estimate variously the possibility of increasing existing varieties of food and introduce, frequently in a highly speculative manner, interesting possibilities of food from the sea and crops without soil, or by harnessing atomic and solar energy. We cannot let ourselves be led down these attractive byways at the moment. We are concerned with the problem all this poses for the Church.

It is a problem, of course, which we, sheltering under the even now bountiful aegis of the British economy, hardly begin to see. We can always go along to the grocer's and get our supplies. But the Asian peasant rarely has a super-market handy. And the Indian peasant hasn't any money with which to buy—the average income in India is £20 a year. Our Lord pointed out that man shall not live by bread alone but he also made sure of feeding five thousand people when they were hungry and commended the giving of a cup of water to his little ones.

It is largely—but not wholly—because of this hunger that the Church faces a new creation that most church-people have unfortunately not even dreamed about as yet —industrialised Asian man, about whom the adjective "underprivileged" hovers so unhappily.

Whatever else may be said about the People's China, it is certain that they have fully accepted the idea of industrialisation. India is now busily engaged on its second Five-Year Plan in the course of which it will spend £4,725 million on development. Even so, it has been creating new jobs at the rate of only four million a year, while the new job-seekers have been increasing at the rate of seven million a year. Japan is once more competing with the west in world markets. Even Tristan da Cunha, for the first time in the history of this "loneliest island in the world," now has its fish-canning industry—and the resulting problems have not been few.

The Church is not primarily concerned with industry as such. But it is inescapably involved in what industry does to those who are made in the image of God. Can we begin to see what this is?

Industry depends on labour, even in these days of automation. And so it takes a man from a rural community where his whole life has been lived in the comparative safety of his tribal connections and where his actions and routine have been geared to the rhythm of nature and transforms him into a creature without roots. It takes the cottager who learnt something of God from the roses round his door and puts him in a great block of flats—someone has described such buildings as "human filing cabinets." Industry creates a new frontier between a man and the things with which he had long been familiar. And it can leave him a midget bewildered by giant machines. Is it any wonder that such an engulfed creature grasps desperately at any straw and lands in his millions in worship at the feet of a film star or baseball player, or, less innocently, in the arms of a raucous demagogue?

Yet so attractive are the fruits of industry that men willingly subject themselves to its lure. And, let it not be forgotten, it is industry which has helped to increase the life-span of hitherto starving peasants.

One of the most evil effects of industry is this tendency to put men in great heaps. Ten years or so ago gold was found in a previously uninhabited area of the Orange Free States. Hundreds of square miles of bare earth rapidly became covered with townships, housing people from a multitude of nations. In one district alone the population has swollen from 700 to 310,000—thus multiplying 433 times! Think what that would mean in terms of supplying new church buildings in your town, where you wouldn't have the additional problems an African population has to face.

The major portion of this increased population consists of Africans. Forced to find a polltax or bewitched by thoughts of glittering cities they have left their kraals and

47

so often have left their full manhood and gone to become grubbing ants. The temptations to vice are obvious for vice is boon companion of money. Many of those Africans had been brought to Christ in childhood and had continued as faithful Christians. But so far Christian bodies have been able to do little to provide the means of grace in these teeming locations where such means are more than ever necessary.

Or take Guiana. The British Government has authorised the expenditure of some 44,000,000 dollars on development. The result is that new settlements have been set up in what was not long since virgin bush. Regular church attendants from places like Georgetown have been set down in the kind of raw new communities which cause such major headaches even in the United Kingdom. We are familiar with the problems of building a community sense in the new housing areas which dot this country. We have two thousand years of tradition behind us. What are the chances in Guiana? Has the Church a word for those who have been thus uprooted or must it preserve an embarrassed silence? Where is it to get the funds to provide new missionaries, new buildings in such places?

Nor are such population movements the only ones which concern us. For one reason or another there are constant mass treks. In Fiji Indians form more than half the population. In Ceylon there are nearly a million Indians and a similar number in Malaya. Mauritius has a quarter of a million, while there are enormous Indian colonies in Durban, Jamaica, Trinidad, Guiana and many other places. What is the missionary to do in Guiana, "land of six peoples?" Is he to concentrate on the East Indians or the Amerindians or the Chinese or those of negro descent or the Europeans (of many varieties)? He cannot tackle them all. Yet the Church's commission is to them all.

48

A similar problem arises with the Chinese—there are supposed to be some twenty million of them outside mainland China. They are to be found in many places. They are the crack in the bamboo curtain. Yet what is the Church to do in a place like Malaya? Is it to try to work equally with Chinese, Indian, Malay and European? Is each missionary to speak four languages, become familiar with four sets of customs, four different backgrounds? How can he become "identified" with four different nationalities at once? How can the same man be across four frontiers at once?

Perhaps there is a good example of what this means in a current difficulty in the diocese of Singapore. The time has come when an Asian should be raised to the status of a bishop in this diocese (which includes Malaya). There are a number of worthy Asians. But if the status is given to a Chinese, how will the Indians feel? And vice versa. And if the status were conferred upon an Indian and a Chinese at the same time, would this lead at any future date to a Chinese Anglican diocese in Singapore and an Indian Anglican diocese in the same place? Perhaps such questions are a domestic problem, with their interest limited to Anglicans only. But they surely illustrate the fact that the Church does not have to deal with a humanity neatly sorted into appropriate bundles, each ready to be evangelised according to the book of rules. And they illustrate that our word "frontiers" has little to do with the geographical demarcation adorned with customs posts.

Such movements of population are to some degree the result of "natural" causes. But what of those pitiful people who because of war and persecution sit and weep by some strange Babylonian waters? Australia recently welcomed its millionth immigrant since the war. Many of them have been refugees. Bishop Stephen Neill has described Christian service to refugees and displaced persons as perhaps the most successful piece of ecumenical work since the war. The World Council of Churches has achieved the steady movement of some 12,000 refugees a year to new homes beyond the seas. But this creates problems as well as helps suffering people.

How far should the Church treat these people as national units in their new countries? How far should religious services be provided in their familiar languages? How far should they be encouraged to become integrated in their new surroundings? Bishop Neill suggests that because Norwegian, Swedish and other Lutherans began their lives in Chicago with services in their own languages, even though they all now use English "it might be possible in a square mile of Chicago to find six Lutheran churches of different origin, hardly varying in doctrine or emphasis but with no fellowship beyond that of personal goodwill and co-operation."

Here, of course, the Romans have an advantage. When Greeks or Italians go to live in South Wales or New South Wales, they can give the same degree of intelligent attention to the Mass as they could in their former homes. But is that an adequate argument for man's highest activity, worship, being carried on in a language he does not understand? Doesn't the Roman solution merely bypass the problem?

There have, of course, been such population movements all through the ages. But never before have they been so accelerated by factors like the ease of travel and the devastations left by worldwide war. In any case, we are not here concerned with a historical assessment of what the Church has done in the past about refugees and exiles. It needs all our efforts to try to find out what is the will of God for us at this moment. What is he calling us to do?

We know that basically we are called to give ourselves unstintingly to the fullest realisation of man-in-relationship with God and therefore with his fellows but where on earth (for we are firmly implanted on that planet, wherever our ideas may run), where on earth do we begin?

Of course, it would be quite hopeless if we were just at the beginning. We are the inheritors of the Christian sacrifice of the ages. We are living after the "Great Century" of missions and can garner its fruits. We are living in the age which Professor Latourette characterises as the day of "advance through storm."

The storms of this century have removed many of the old familiar landmarks. They have disturbed ancient patterns of population. They have been accompanied by a transformation of the old political frameworks. Throughout their turbulences there have been the frequent lightning flashes of a new scientific development which has altered standards of living. And, above all, the storms have roused an Asia lost in centuries of sleep.

Such furies of the elements have created new gaping cracks in the face of mankind. They have left us with frontiers which, as each issue of a daily newspaper abundantly proves, are expanding before our eyes.

Humanly speaking, the scene is frightening. How can we carry on the Christian battle faced with such hosts of Midian? There is only one answer. We must return to the source of our true strength, the things of the Spirit. It is then that we learn that man is a fundamentally religious animal. It is his highest attribute. But because man is a fallen creature he has also found his highest attribute a source of his most grievous divisions. Religions are frontiers.

Chapter 5

Which war against the soul

EVEN in the twentieth century, man is fundamentally a religious animal. He must be because he is made in the image of God. Even the rootless machine-minder, pursuing a monochrome existence in "a subtopia which spreads like mildew," has moments when he finds the film star and the welfare state unsatisfying. Perhaps such moments occur when his child dies or on the rare occasions when he sees a sunset, but occur they do.

The industrialisation of Asian man has been accompanied by a resurgence of his ancient religions, though to express it in this way is to over-simplify. There are many other factors involved in this resurgence, not least the phenomena of contemporary nationalisms. But that more and more people seem to be finding a need for a spiritual basis in life seems undeniable.

In May 1954 thousands of Buddhist monks from many countries met in Rangoon. Their meeting place had cost a fortune to construct and was a replica of the cave in which Gautama the Buddha had lived. This was only the sixth such Buddhist conference in the 2,500 years of their history—which indicates its significance. It was planned to last two whole years—what a contrast with the go-getting western world which attempted to include two major conferences, Evanston and Minneapolis, in a couple of weeks. The aim of the Buddhist conference was a complete revision of their holy writings and a careful reorganisation of their missionary strategy. This in itself is startling, for Buddhism has been a world-denying religion, yet here it is actively seeking to conquer the world. But much more startling, and utterly shaming for any Christian, is the argument they have evolved. "Christianity," they say, "is a religion of the West. All wars start in the West. Therefore Christianity is a cause of wars. Be a Buddhist and thus help to ensure world peace."

How many professing Christians in this country could cheerfully undertake to refute such an argument? The average man-in-the-pew would need much more instruction than he usually seems to have. He must understand the heart of the Faith before he can disprove the Buddhist assertion that love, the aim of the Christian, is itself a form of desire and all desire leads to strife. The only peace, says the Buddhist, comes through the extinction of desire. But even if the average man fully understood true Christian doctrine he would have sorrowfully to admit the facts of western wars and the impression they leave on eastern minds.

The Buddhists have called their meeting place "The Pagoda of World Peace." It is quite idle to deny the emotional attraction of this for a world grown weary of carnage and cowering under the hydrogen bomb.

Now this Buddhist philosophy is having its effect, not merely in the East. London has its Buddhist Society and it is making gains—a London bank clerk recently became a Buddhist priest. America has 63,000 Buddhists. If Buddhism can make converts from our two-thousand year tradition, what of the newer Christians of Burma, Ceylon, Thailand and other countries? It would be faithless to imply that the grace of God is anywhere finally overcome. But it would be a sin against that grace to do less than recognise how feeble have been our efforts to be fellow-workers with God in the Buddhist world and the task Christianity has there. The increasing number of saffron robes are grim warnings.

Were Buddhism the only resurgent foe of Christianity it might be possible for the Church to concentrate much greater energies at this point. But what of Islam?

For over a thousand years Christians have been asking that question. In our generation it becomes more urgent still. On a world map Islam is a great black crescent spreading from West Africa through the Middle East and Pakistan down through the Malay Peninsula into South East Asia (and don't forget the mosques at Woking, Cardiff Newcastle, and so on). This crescent covers most of our twentieth century tinder points. It embraces most of the great centres of oil, essential spirit of our machine age. And Islamic countries have acquired a political power in our day which enables them not only to dictate terms to the rest of the world but also to acquire the sort of prestige which made nineteenth century Europe dominant. Surely there is a warning finger for Christendom here?

But apart from the growing power of Islam in its political relationships, what of the individual Muslim?

He finds himself part of a great brotherhood, the contemporary success of which vindicates for him its ancient tenets. He is exuberant. But he may well become more exuberant still, for those who guide his faith are learning to put Muhammad's wine into new bottles. There are astonishing parallels between the refurbished Islam of our day and many movements in Christianity. Bishop Stephen Neill has listed them:

(1) There is the return to the Koran itself, a "back-to-the-Bible" movement.

(2) The desert prophet of seventh century Arabia is being changed into the ideal of modern democratic man.

(3) There is a willingness to submit Islam to a very thorough reinterpretation. For example, Muhammad's permission to have four wives at a time is not denied but it is brought nearer to modern monogamy by emphasising that Muhammad insisted they all be treated equally. Since no man can treat four wives equally, then obviously no man can have four wives.

(4) There is a serious attempt to relate traditional Muslim law with the conditions of our day.

A streamlined Islam has acquired political power. But even now we have not seen its final strength. This lies in the individual Muslim, for the average Muslim-on-his-prayer-mat seems a more committed person than the Christian-in-his-pew—or out of it. The Muslim has no embarrassment about saying his prayers in public when the Muezzin calls. The Muslim, wherever he finds himself, remains not only a Muslim but a proselytising Muslim. An obvious Englishman—or rather, Welshman—was approached in Cardiff docks the other day with the words "Why are you a Christian? I am a Muslim, let me tell you why."

Islam is the faith of men who with new political power are increasingly travelling and making contacts. Remember that Islam knows no colour bar and that the colour bar is the twentieth century's most urgent problem. Remember that Islam is the faith of the merchants who spread across North and West Africa and they never leave their convictions at home. It has been suggested that Islam conquers because it allows an easy code of behaviour. Be that as it may, we have to get down much more seriously to knowing not only what the Muslim world believes but also where Christianity can out-think, out-pray and out-live it. We can never become oblivious to the shattering fact that Islam is later than Christianity in time, that Muhammad knew something, however distorted, about Christ, that Islam went through the heart of the Christian world like a well-tempered scimitar. Islam may have gained much of its conquest by the sword but it did at least succeed in converting most of those who held the sword.

For all the success of Islam, Christ's command to preach to all men remains supreme. And the position is far from hopeless. "I gather that Muslims in India today are in more favourable mood to listen," the Anglican Metropolitan, himself an Indian, recently told his Diocesan Council.

Just ten years ago there emerged a new factor in world politics. For the first time in history there was a united, self-governing India. Deliberately and with no small success India has pursued a policy of neutralism between the two great power blocs. It is a policy which brings prestige in the eyes of peoples who above all want to feel they are making up their own minds about their country's future. The Indian Government has asserted on more than one occasion its intention of abiding by the freedom of religion which is written into its Constitution. Indian leaders have referred to Christianity in most friendly terms. Mr. Nehru himself has frequently asserted the rights of Christianity in India. Christianity is both the third largest and the third oldest religion in India. Yet there are something less than three Christians (whether Roman Catholic or otherwise) out of every hundred Indians. Mostly these Christians are grouped in comparatively small areas. In many cases they are drawn from the least educated and poorest sections of the population. And some have become as casual about the Faith as some of us.

Has Hinduism anything to fear from such opposition? It would appear that it feels it has.

There were many Hindus who, before 1947, felt that

once the British Raj went, Christianity would go with it. They have been disappointed to find that the number of Christians continues to grow. This is most abhorrent to them for they feel that every Hindu who is converted reduces the strength of the Hindu community both politically and otherwise. Furthermore, they feel that Christianity is basically destructive. Their own faith allows all sorts of religions both to exist and to absorb whatever bits one approves in other religions. "Thou shalt have none other gods . . ." is to them merely an arrogant assertion.

So there come home the tales of persecution of Christians, the difficulties of evangelism, the problems of staffing and a hundred other woes. And when an Indian statesman suggests that Christian missionaries from the west are no longer wanted, some people too rapidly leap to conclusions. An examination of Indian Government statements on the entry of missionaries shows that the Government has done no more than reserve the right to exclude some missionaries, which is perfectly reasonable in theory and has, so far at least, been used completely reasonably in practice. That no European should be invited to do a job which an Indian could do equally well, that no European should enter the country to control men who are his peers, spiritually and also mentally, are fair demands. And even more fair are the demands that no "missionary" should use his position to create purely political problems for a Government which in any case has enough problems already. There have been people who have gone into India and other countries under the guise of missionaries and have proceeded to settle down in delicately balanced areas, like the border of Kashmir, and propagate doctrines somewhat remote from the Gospel. India must not be judged because, as an adult State, she claims the right to control such people.

Nor must we who are outside India judge India's re-action to Christianity by any implications such statements may have. India's Minister of Health, with cabinet rank, ever since 1947, has been a remarkable Christian lady. Last Christmas the *Times of India,* whose editor is not a Christ-ian, printed a magnificently Christian Christmas supple-ment. The reputation which Christians acquired for their wonderful works of love at the frontiers when so many people needed Christian love in 1947, have not been for-gotten. Was it not Mr. Gandhi, who was not a Christian, who sent a telegram to Hindus and Muslims asking them to "be Christians to one another"? And when that same Gandhi was assassinated, thousands of non-Christians in India said he died a "Christ-like death", the highest com-pliment they could pay.

All those things are true. Yet they must not conceal the fact that there is in India today a militant, resurgent Hindu-ism. Nor does Hinduism limit its activities to India. In places like Guiana, Trinidad and the South Sea Islands, all of them a long way from India, the big Indian population has seen to it that they are well equipped with Hindu temples and do much to propagate their faith, especially among those Indians who show any signs of becoming de-Indianised.

Buddhism, Islam and Hinduism have long been spoken of among the "great" religions of the world. The same thing cannot be said for the more primitive religions of Africa. But to assume that this means that they offer no con-temporary challenge to Christianity would be folly. They too show signs of reinvigoration. What other explanation is there for ritual murders and increased recourse to witch-doctory? Where do ancient religions find their place in the horrors of Mau Mau? Uganda has long been regarded as one of Africa's most Christian countries, yet today it is much afflicted by a very lively paganism. And there is the recently much-publicised "Alice Movement" in the Copper Belt and the Kitawala in the Belgian Congo.

You don't have to look far in Africa to see new frontiers arise as a revolt against the white man takes different forms. And, after all, if you were an African and you saw what a professedly Christian government in South Africa is doing to Africans, merely because they are Africans, what would you think? Perhaps the greatest evil resulting from *apartheid* lies in the fact that the whole non-European world is judging the West (the so-called Christian West) by what is happening in buses and parks in the Union of South Africa. The relationship between South Africa's deliberate dehumanising of the Bantu and the anti-west remarks at the Bandung conference is not far to seek.

But it is Africa as a whole which brings to mind another religious phenomenon of our day. It is the rise of sects. There have always been sects and heresies but never before, perhaps, have they shown the sort of vigour that they do today. Africa is supposed to have some six hundred of them. They pursue their thrusting way in tiny islands like St. Helena and across the hinterland of vast Australia, not to mention America. Their devotees have an enthusiasm which mocks Christians of more sober schools of thought. Young Mormons, for example, have little future in their own community unless, when still young, they are prepared to give at least a year's service at their own expense as Mormon missionaries. Many of these sects are concerned only with "sheep-stealing"—they make their inroads on those who already know something of Christ, rather than tackle the harder task of the completely unevangelised.

These sects, to some minds, pose a problem of ecumenical thinking which perhaps some ecumenical thinkers have not yet formulated. Our day has been rightly described as the great era of Christian fellowship as expressed in efforts towards reunion through the Ecumenical Movement. Our day is also a great era of vigorous new sects and reinvigorated old ones. Is there a connection between those two facts? Is there something in ecumenicity which stimulates sects? Do the fringers cater for something in humanity which resists the fuller fellowship? Is Satan himself making greater than ever efforts as our Lord's design that they "may all be one" becomes nearer realisation? Is it possible that the Church has become over-concerned with institutionalism and formalism, thus irking some who prize liberty? Should we seriously reconsider our own presentation of Christianity?

Whatever the answers may be, they are important for they should show us, or at least make us seek, the way over the frontiers which exist between Christians themselves. And they may even help to lower the frontier barriers between Christianity and other religions.

But we cannot leave this chapter until we have mentioned one more frontier. It is the variously described way of thought and action known as Communism, which has deliberately established a gulf between itself and Christianity. Is it possible in a short compass to write of Communism? Is Communism the same thing in Russia, China and Poland? Does a Communist leaflet in Tibet say the same sort of thing as the *Daily Worker*?

We cannot begin to analyse Communism in our available space but we must recognise two facts. Basically Communism is opposed to Christianity and, secondly, it has for the hungry peasant of Asia and Africa the lure that a rich bookmaker has for the man who stands in a dole queue. The bookmaker's stomach is full. The Church has a great deal of thinking and praying to do about those who see on their pennies merely the image of Caesar and forthwith render all things to him.

The Church has yet to solve the problems of crossing frontiers established when false gods set up their Kingdoms in the soul of man.

Chapter 6

Devout Men Out of Every Nation

THERE are two completely opposite tendencies visible
in the world at the present time. One is the increasing
splitting which gives us nationalisms. The other is the increasing growth of the worldwide Church which, for all its
weaknesses, is a fact and leads to unity.

When Chesterton wrote *The Napoleon of Notting Hill
Gate* he no doubt felt he was making an enormous joke.
That one part of London should ever declare its independence and take up arms against another was purest fantasy.
London, at least at the time of writing, is still fairly united.
But Chesterton's fancy has almost become our fact. In Wales
you will see "England keep out" on railway bridges, while
in Scotland "Englishmen : Go home" beguiles the traveller.
The same process prevails across the world. Is it modern
man's defiant assertion that he does not want to become
submerged by some juggernaut of world standardisation?

On the first page of his most important book, *Christianity
and the Asian Revolution*, the Lutheran Bishop R. B.
Manikam says, "In 1954 Winston Churchill proclaimed,
with all the eloquence at his command, 'I did not become
His Majesty's Prime Minister to preside over the liquida-
tion of the British Empire'. Today India, Pakistan, Burma,
Ceylon, Indonesia and the Philippines are independent
nations." Parts of Africa, Malaya, Singapore, the Middle
East have followed the same path and others stand
impatiently at the gate.

Now let it be said immediately that many of the nations which acquired such freedom are today in a happier than ever relationship with their former overlords. That doesn't alter the fact that a worldwide splitting up is taking place. "Fission" is characteristic not only of the atom. The only political system which is forever adding to those chained to its orbit is Communism—and the means by which Russia adds to its minions and the way it subsequently treats them is not likely to endear "colonialism" to anyone.

Before the old-fashioned colonialism passes from our memories we might pause and pay some of the tributes it deserves. Today Zanzibar Cathedral stands on the site of the old slave market. How much longer would slavery have lasted had Zanzibar been left to its own devices or the tender mercies of Arab traders? Today the West Indies would be even more poverty stricken had its sugar trade not been developed. India would be even less equipped for the modern world had not John Company spent money there; Malaya would not have had its rubber and its tin might still be hidden underground. The colonial administrator may still appear in cartoons as a wicked monster but many of them were men of high vocation. The existence of today's Commonwealth Conferences show that people who were once colonial do not regard the fact as permanent justification for enmity.

But we are not concerned with a defence of imperialism, for Christianity is tied to no emperor's chariot. Our job is to face the fact that the world has split into nation states and that many of them are even more embittered because they have in the past received benefits. Giving is sometimes a more difficult process than receiving. As a thinking American said the other day, "We have a foolishly large number of dollars and we want to share them with people who have none. But it seems that the more we give away the

63

more they dislike us. Perhaps it demands even more grace to give than it does to accept." Virgil had a word for it long ago. "I fear the Greeks, especially when they bear gifts."

But before we go trying to find deep motives for the unwillingness of Asian states to accept what the West offers them, before we write them off as hopelessly unco-operative, let us remember one type of thing the West does offer. It offers many cans of Hollywood film. Can India be described as anti-American simply because it has decreed that no American films can be imported without permission? Has not the Orient a right to protect its peoples from many of the standards which Hollywood purveys? Can we condemn a country because it feels that it might manage to get along without Coca Cola?

But to leave it at that is to treat the matter too flippantly. Few of us can begin to imagine the intensity of the hatred which we have generated in Asian and African minds. Even those who have done so much to help are put in the same category as others. A friendly African Christian told the Bishop of Johannesburg, famous for his championship of the African cause, "When we have been driven too far and the streets flow with blood, your blood will mingle with the rest." There is certainly an unreasonable element in the hatred of the once have-nots for the once-haves. We must therefore the more seriously ask what are we, in this new situation, trying to pass on to the rest of the world?

It was Hermann Goering who alleged that every time he heard the word "culture" he reached for his gun. The deflated twentieth century has a similar attitude about the word "civilisation." We have become so frightened by our own civilisation that we are doubtful about spreading it. In any case, what do we want to spread? Are we merely trying to make the strip comic a worldwide phenomenon? Do we wish to plant existentialism in Car Nicobar? Are the habits of a stockbroker in Surrey to be taken as the pattern for a sugar labourer in Suva? The people of the Belgian Congo can be non-U and still be Christians.

As long as overseas nationalisms assert no more than a claim that Dayaks shall grow up as Dayaks and not as pale reflections of Europeans, surely they will have our fullest agreement. We are not concerned with passing on English etiquette. It was such a motive which powered the needles of those who knitted black woolly socks or sewed flannel petticoats for equatorial Africans.

The Church stands for the individuality of each human being. Each is equal in the sight of God. Each is of equal worth. Cannot the same thing be true about nations? Bishop Westcott's remark that the final commentary on St. John's Gospel will be written by an Indian must always be remembered. Who can doubt that the long centuries of mystical thought which have been the heritage of the privileged among India's peoples will one day make a rich jewel in the crown of Christ? It is enough to remind ourselves of the existence of Sadhu Sundar Singh. Who can doubt that the glorious childlikeness of the African has its special place in the heart of a Saviour who said, "Except ye become like little children. . . ." And what have the Japanese, so quick to learn, so capable of assimilation, and the Chinese with their eternal patience and sense of the infinite, to add to the spiritual riches of the Church? Is there any nation which will not one day lay at the feet of the Lamb a treasure which no other nation could produce?

The Church does not have to condemn nationalisms except in so far as they become nationalisms at the expense of other nations, except in so far as they become enlarge-

ments of the selfishness and self-willedness of an individual.
Nor, indeed, does the Church have to fear national religions. They do not have to be annihilated. They have to
be fulfilled. And who can doubt that the Spirit who through
the Church sanctified the glory that was Greece and the
grandeur that was Rome and added them to the God-
possessedness which was Israel is capable of fulfilling yet
more gloriously Islam or Buddhism or Hinduism?

It is worth remembering that Protestant missions in
India were begun by a German Lutheran, sponsored by
the King of Denmark and supported by an Anglican
Society. Three individual sovereign nations were concerned.
The Church can accept nationalisms but it cannot accept
what they all too readily become—ends in themselves.

How then can we who are the Church in the West
begin to disarm the suspicions of the nations who make up
the rest of the world and show that in proclaiming the
Gospel we are not trying to put them into spiritual or
any other kind of tutelage?

There is one lesson which we have barely begun to
learn. And the time when we shall be examined in its
meaning draws near.

We have barely begun to learn that we have as much to
receive from the younger Churches as to give.

The picture of a self-styled Lady Bountiful dressed in
European skirts and patronisingly dispensing Christ Crucified to heathen who bow down to wood and stone was
always a blasphemy. But some of us have been slow to
realise it.

Perhaps the reader will forgive a personal experience.
When the Society for the Propagation of the Gospel had
its 250th Birthday, it built a replica of the ship in which
its first missionary sailed—*Centurion*. On that replica
sailed teams of African, Indian, Pakistani, Dayak, West

Indian and other priests. They disembarked at eighty-five United Kingdom ports and preached the Gospel to English holiday makers and any who happened to be willing to listen. The greatest lesson S.P.G. staff learnt from the Birthday was the spiritual power of those visitors. Their very existence justified two and a half centuries of effort. Their message to this country laid up a great reservoir of strength for the next two and a half centuries.

Were such an experience unique it would not be worth quoting. But it is not. Every missionary organisation which has brought overseas visitors to this country can testify to the blessings they have left behind them on their return.

More and more we have got to learn—and have got to show that we have learnt—that the world Mission of the Church is a two-way process. There is no country which cannot give and no country which can afford not to receive. The very sight of an Indian or African face in an English pulpit is a tangible expression of the "great things the Lord is doing" in our day. And was not that the theme of the most powerful sermons in the *Acts of the Apostles*? When, as is so frequently the case, the message which leaves those Indian or African lips is a word of *power* showing infinite love of the Word himself, can there be greater testimony to the equality of all men in the sight of God?

Today we hear quite a lot about bringing leading indigenous clergy to this country for further training and experience. There are many dangers in such a process. Such men may get lost between the two worlds of East and West. And if such a process is linked to the much canvassed "training of future leaders" theories, it might fall entirely athwart the Christian conception of servanthood rather than leadership. In any case, the whole thing is shot through with the dangerous assumption that they are coming merely to receive. But if only we can get it into our heads that they are coming to give us something, then it must not only bring joy in heaven but also remove dangerous suspicions of a superior-to-inferior relationship on earth. Those who are familiar with the experiment of St. Augustine's College, Canterbury, which is now the Central College of the Anglican Communion and houses Anglicans from many nations for short periods, suggest that the most important development is not that Indians and Africans go away capable of taking further diplomas or degrees but that they go away knowing their own solidarity as Christians. And in their spare moments, few as they are, they have been able to show English stay-at-homes something of God's greater family.

If only we could get all this across in a clear voice to the younger Churches they would know we regard them as partners, not children, thus removing not a few suspicions. How much stronger they would be in the face of their nationalisms. They could finally controvert ideas of spiritual colonialisms.

But it is not only in sermons at home that we can look to the younger Churches for help. They have many other lessons for us.

Think, for example, of a country where a man has been allowed numerous wives. In a polygamous society the missionary Church is brought face to face with the basic facts of the relationship between man and woman. Is monogamy merely a western convention which arose because the sexes were roughly equal in number? Is there any final reality about it? Does the Gospel mean anything when it talks about the twain becoming one flesh or is it being a bit romantic? Has God so made a man and a woman that only by adhering for life to one partner can they both learn something of and share in his mystery of creation? Missionaries who have worked for long periods in a polygamous society throw a great deal of light on the Christian answer to these questions. But their answer must be incomplete compared with the answer of one whose tradition has been polygamous, who has been brought up to accept it as natural. Such a man really knows what polygamy means, what effect it has on the status of women, how it affects the security of children and so on. He can approach the Christian doctrine of marriage with a fresh mind and a lucidity which is perhaps denied to us. The younger churches have much to teach us of marriage. And if any denies our need to learn, let him remember our divorce figures.

Then again, the Church overseas is faced by something which our Christianised society can usually succeed in overlooking. What is really meant by conversion? Those who have grown up in the Christian Faith rarely have to ask themselves such a question. For them the difference between being a Christian and not being one may become very blurred. How different for one who becomes a member of a numerically tiny Church in a pagan land. He sees the difference very clearly. The younger Churches will increasingly teach us much about membership. And who will deny that an England where so many babies are baptised and so few reach mature Christian stature does not need to learn such a lesson?

And what about money? It is significant that when World Christian Books wanted to include this subject in its notable series it went to an Indian—Azariah. Does giving money merely mean the chink of a coin on an alms dish? Is there a true relationship between earning and giving? Is the gift of a coin symbolic or an end in itself? Does it mark the surrender of all God's world—which in our case would include the slums of an industrial town and in the case of an African the thatch of his kraal and all that goes on underneath it?

But, thinking of India, is there not a still more important gift a younger Church has given to an older? Has not the great move towards unity which is the Church of South India given a great stimulus to us to give more thought and prayer towards such matters here at home? It was a missionary conference at Madras in 1902 which was the precedent for the famous Edinburgh Conference of 1910 (from which the publishers of this book have drawn their name). And how much in the way of international and inter-Church co-operation stems from that?

There are so many questions on which we await the complementary experience of the younger Churches. One day, no doubt, someone will get down to it and compile the great tome which is always being talked about in mission houses, the symposium of the wisdom of the world Church collated from its various backgrounds.

It is not only along these lines that we look for guidance. We also look to the younger Churches for further light on the soul of man. What about those brought up in the reality of witch-doctory and devil worship, will they not have something to say about the powers of Satan? Will they not more fully map the kingdom of evil?

In this realm of the mind and soul one cannot omit mention of art. Western man has played fast and loose with art and has turned it into a frustrating means of self-expression which rarely has any message to communicate to other selves. What is the connection between art and truth? Is there anything in the statement of a Cyrene (Southern Rhodesia) boy, "I will paint it and then it will be true"? Quite certainly the art which comes from places like Cyrene, a mission school where African boys have developed into world famous artists, has much to add to the world's cultural heritage. For there they have not lost sight of the fact that art is a perfect harmonising of work and worship, of hand and soul. The art of Cyrene is an offering to God because all life is lived in the presence of God—thereby giving to all life an integrity which is not particularly obvious in the *ateliers* of Chelsea. In Cyrene African boys have been given the materials and told to get on with the job. They have not been allowed to copy European art forms. They have worked in an African vacuum. In insisting on this principle Cyrene has asserted that the Church is concerned with developing fully-grown Africans, not pale reflections of Europeans. But it has done more than that. It has re-taught the West—yes, us in the West —something of the purposes of art.

Across the world the Church is being the patron of painting and music and sculpture and architecture, of all the expressions of man's love for beauty which the Church has nurtured in Europe. This process has begun, but only barely and in many cases it is possible that it has started off on the wrong foot and must retrace its steps and begin again. But may we not look forward to a day when an Asian Handel or Dante or Leonardo da Vinci lifts up our hearts anew and more richly to the Throne? To suggest that in all these things the work of the Church can be restricted by nationalisms is to imply that Dante could have no meaning outside his own country or age.

The Church is always giving and receiving across all the national frontiers, though so many Church people have yet to become aware of the fact.

But there is also another facet which is more hidden but none the less important. Getting up time and going to bed time are particularly times of prayer for Christians. Around the world the sun rises and sets at different times, covering every twenty-four hours every day of the year. The exist-

ence of a worldwide Christian Church means that prayer
for the worldwide Christian Church is constantly being
offered. There was a time when the incessant worship of
God depended on the ministry of angels. Now men join in
too. And who can estimate the importance of that fact in
the developing pattern of God's plan for all mankind?

> As o'er each continent and island
> The dawn brings on another day,
> The voice of prayer is never silent
> Nor dies the strain of praise away.

When John Ellerton wrote those words over half a century ago, they were just beginning to be true. Today they
are a proclamation that stands unbowed before all the
assaults of paganism and nationalisms. And if only we
could say that to the football crowds who sentimentally
sing those words at Cup Finals and the Asians who feel so
weak in the face of alien philosophies, how much we should
have accomplished.

Christians don't lack the words to say in this fractious
world. But they all too often lack the courage or the vision
to say them.

The Church transcends nationalisms because all nations
become one in prayer and the Church transcends nationalisms because God is not colour conscious when he chooses
his prophets. The world gives a picture of constantly expanding frontiers but there is also the parallel picture of
the Church with the duty of and potentiality for crossing
them all. We have a more blood-stirring challenge than any
Davy Crockett.

CHAPTER 7

That We Might Gain the More

NOWHERE in the Bible are we given any authority for counting heads. Nowhere in the formularies of the Church can such authority be discerned. It is true that clergy and ministers are from time to time called upon to fill in some form or other indicating the number of communicants they have served in the past year or something but many have a suspicion that such forms, once completed, are rarely seen again.

It is true that in the *Acts of the Apostles* we are once or twice told how many people were added to the Church in one day but they seem to have given up the counting habit fairly rapidly.

Today, when the highly trained mathematicians who have become the ultimate symbol of mechanised man— statisticians—seem able to ascertain the number of babies born with six fingers or pear-shaped birthmarks or any other odd calculation you might desire (the only place where such information seems useful is in radio quiz games), one thing and one thing alone defeats them. They are unable to tell us how many Christians there are in the world.

And that, to some people, would appear to be a joyful proof of the greatness of Christianity.

Speaking quite seriously, however, how can anyone begin to assess the number of Christians in the world? What are the standards of judgment to be? The number of baptised? The number of adherents? The number who attend church once a Sunday, once a month? Would similar criteria satisfy both Baptists and Roman Catholics? In any case, can anyone assess the degree of Christian conviction in his best friend? Or even of his very own self?

It is quite impossible to produce statistics of the number of Christians in the world. It is quite impossible to indicate with any finality how the number of today's Christians compares with the number of Christians a century ago. And perhaps that is something which is in any case best left enshrouded in the mysteries of God. For we are told to preach. We are not told to convert. And if our responsibility ends at preaching—reminding ourselves of the fullest meaning of that word in thought and deed as well as in speech—then we do not have to get hypnotised by numbers.

On the other hand, we are human. We want to know, so to speak, who is winning. So we keep on asking for some assurance as to how the battle is going. Keeping in mind the last few paragraphs and remembering that the greater part of the Church is in any case invisible, let us turn to Dr. Latourette—who is well aware of the imponderables of Christianity.

Most people would give Dr. K. S. Latourette, Professor of Missions and Oriental History at Yale, what the Americans call a very high rating as a missionary historian. His epic work in seven volumes, published in 1944, has as the title of its last volume *Advance through Storm*. The period dealt with is 1914 to 1944 and covers the Great War and its greater successor. Never, says Dr. Latourette, had the human race so clearly been on the march. Patterns of culture were being reshaped and cultures once most closely associated with Christianity were receding. Development of government control in various countries had decreased the freedom of the individual which was the basis of Protestant-

ism. Over everything hung the havoc of war and the super-
ficialities of the short-skirted Eton-cropped twenties and
the hunger marches of the thirties.

Yet Latourette asserts that in 1944 Christianity was a
more potent world factor than in 1914. He even goes so
far as to describe the thirty years under consideration as
"one of the great ages of faith". Stop and think of that.
You who are middle-aged have lived through what one of
the greatest of Christian historians, surveying the whole
Christian era, calls "one of the great ages of faith." Such a
title, he says, can be justified when measured by criteria of
geographic extent and also by the vigour of Christians
themselves. Numerical losses in Europe had been made
good by increased spiritual force. Percentages of Christians
in non-Occidental lands had doubled in the period. In 1914
the non-Occident had depended on the Churches of the
West. By 1944 much of the leadership and support was
indigenous. For the first time in history Christianity had
become worldwide and not merely an imperial extension.
No other religion, says Latourette, has ever embraced such
worldwide dimensions. It was notable, too, how in this
period Christians were becoming increasingly conscious of a
world fellowship. Protestant Christianity, he says, was developing more rapidly and with greater influence than
Roman in the period. Christianity, Latourette concludes,
has been more widely influential after 1914 than ever
before. Here indeed frontiers are being crossed even as they
expand.

Professor Latourette has written quite a few books since
that date. In none of them has he seen it necessary to go
back on those opinions. He does not suggest for one moment
that such progress must inevitably be maintained. Rather
his whole study of Christian history leads him to the conclusion that Christian advance is like the incoming tide.

Each wave goes a little further than its predecessors but there is an ebb in between.

We are apt to regard the end of the great missionary era as occurring not long after Queen Victoria passed. We bewail the poverty of the twentieth century and its effect on missionary giving. We bewail the rising prices with which missionary subscriptions have not kept pace. We bewail a thousand other things. Yet it seems that we are privileged spectators in this great day. Which is the point! Are we spectators and no more? If we are merely shouting on the touchline and letting other people make the efforts, then there is one thought which must make us leap out of our complacency.

No other religion, said Latourette, has ever embraced such worldwide dimensions. And what does St. Matthew report our Lord as saying? "And this gospel shall be preached in all the world for a witness unto all nations; *and then shall the end come.*" If that one text lacked harmony with the rest of the Gospels we might disregard it, though even then at our peril. But it doesn't. Isn't it the counterpart of "God so loved that he sent . . . that all men through him. . . ."?

We are left with a stark fact. In God's plan he has willed it that the consummation of the age, the perfecting of all history, the culmination of all things, the last for which the first was made—how can human words begin to embrace so great a meaning?—will come when those he has charged to preach have done their job.

If we mean what we say "Thy kingdom come, thy will be done on earth . . .", we must preach the Gospel. If we are weary of war and all that divides men, if we tire of vice and all that harms men, if we long for peace and justice and all that heals men, we must preach the Gospel. If we are concerned to see the fulfilment of God's plan, we must preach. With shattering light we see what St. Paul meant "woe unto me if I preach not. . . ." In some dim way we begin to perceive that the woe is not restricted to us but in some awesome way also inflicts itself upon God. Is it possible that we fill up the sufferings of Christ by adding to them by our indifference? But how can we be indifferent when we know what hangs upon our efforts?

What is there that can hinder us? Surely neither principalities nor powers nor things present nor things to come nor nationalisms nor resurgent religions nor economic factors nor cultural bars nor height nor depth nor any other creature. Frontiers there may be but none are unassailable. All those things may be part of the sufferings of this present time but they are not to be compared with the glory that shall be revealed in us. And yet it is not to be revealed in us except in so far as we are in Christ.

It is in this that we see the task and the joy of the Church through the ages. It is for this reason that we have been sent the Comforting Spirit.

But we have reached a dangerous point in our stream of thought. We have reached the rarefied air of the great height and we may suffer a black-out. There is still work to be done and we are God's instruments. We must pass from this mount of Transfiguration back to the valley which would be so grey without the shafts of sunlight which stream down the mountain side. We shall not forget the vision. But neither will we let its radiance blind us to the present reality.

What are the instruments at our disposal for the task God has given us? For the moment we will omit all thoughts of grace and we will assume our spiritual armour is complete. What are the earthly breastplate and sword like?

CHAPTER 8

His Servants Shall Serve Him

M ORE and more people are saying that the parish
system of the Church of England has broken down.

This parish system is not the only one in this country
nor indeed is there any proof it has been the best. The
parallel systems of the Free Churches have many advan-
tages. But in this context they too suffer contemporary dis-
abilities and comparable difficulties, so the Church of
England may well be used as an example.

This system has served so well in the past that few are
going to accept such a breakdown, if fact it be,
lightly. And, in any case, the Church has a genius for
carrying on with an old system, however battered it may
be, until it is discovered that imperceptibly a new system
has taken its place. There are many signs that new systems
are being thought of. Factory chaplains and Butlin's holiday camp chaplains and priest-workers are creatures our
Victorian forebears would have found mystifying.

That doubts should exist at all about the present useful-
ness of the parish system is sufficient proof that there is no
situation which forever remains above criticism. If so well
established an institution has become precarious we must
examine all our institutions. It is perhaps at this point that
the world-wide Church must begin its greatest heartsearch-
ing. The task of proclaiming the Gospel from Britain has
historically been accompanied by the creation of a multi-
plicity of institutions. Schools and hospitals have been the

accepted antennae of the mission station. And let it be pointed out that antennae are not superfluous excrescences but integral parts of the body to which they belong. Schools and hospitals are not only good things in themselves. They are also of vital importance in proclaiming the Kingdom.

Few would have the temerity to question that in a country devoid of education and ignorant of medical services—as have been practically all the countries into which the Church has gone—such deficiencies are the will of a teaching, healing Saviour. But nowadays there are few secular Governments which do not at least include the provision of schools and hospitals in their election programmes. The establishing of an adequate number of such institutions is still a pipe dream in many countries. But numerous governments have at least been alerted to the necessity and that is a fact to the credit of the Church which set the example, even while it decreases needs the Church has formerly met.

Now a strong case can be made out for the deep conviction of many people that however adequately a State provides hospitals, there is still a basic need for Christian counterparts; however complete a State system of education, there is still need for Church schools. Undoubtedly such arguments would prevail on all Christian thinkers if the resources of the Church were boundless. But they are not. Should the Church reconsider its medical and educational work?

It is with no small relief that we announce that we do not intend to attempt a full answer to that question. In its compass this book can only attempt to stimulate thought rather than provide complete answers. But there are one or two points to be made.

There was a time in Britain when all hospitals were

79

Church foundations—the names of London's proudest hospitals still testify to that fact and it is reassuring to find that the State medical service, in renaming some of its old Poor Law and other Institutions, has chosen to confer upon them names suggestive of a Christian outlook. But there are now few hospitals in Britain under specifically Christian control. Having done its work in establishing hospitals in our country, has the Church been right in, for the most part, relinquishing such responsibility? Let it be remarked in passing that there seems to be a happier relationship between the Church and the medical fraternity in this country today than there has been at some periods of our history.

Perhaps the case in respect of Church schools is less clear. All things which involve the mind are less clear than those which involve the body. But again the Church of England is not finding it easy to decide the relative importance of financing schools and finding adequate stipends for its clergy.

But whatever the case may be in England it is quite certain that overseas an institution is the most vulnerable part of the Church's equipment. If ever a hostile Government takes control it is buildings which are likely to be requisitioned. And how many clergy, in countries where education has been taken over by the State, have written confidential letters back to mission houses saying, "At last I don't have to spend half the week keeping school acounts. I can now get on with my real job"?

An Indian priest, writing from near Delhi, says, "Today Rewari has no school, no hospital, no resident priest. Yet the Church is there and never a Sunday passes without the worship of God being offered. The congregation there now is of Rewari. In all there cannot be more than fifty or sixty Anglicans, yet these few look after and care for their church. They pay their annual quota to the diocese and so take their share in its support. They pay five times what they used to when the congregation numbered two hundred or more. They pay the travelling expenses of a priest from Delhi, whereas in the pre-1947 days he received a free pass on the railway. The point of what has been written is not to sing the praises of a parish in the Diocese of Delhi. Rather it is to point to the fact that the Church of Christ in Rewari may be stronger today than it has been during the last sixty years, bereft as it now is of its institutions, which it once had. God's people in Rewari are learning more and more the duty of supporting their church and the privilege that is theirs in maintaining it. Nor are they unmindful that theirs is the responsibility of commending the Faith that is in them to those around them."

The case for or against institutions in a rapidly changing world remains open. But the case for a much greater effort to supply and train living agents has long since been decided. They remain, whatever Government takes office. And it is the blood of the martyrs which has been effective, not the ruins of a Church hospital or even a once magnificent cathedral.

The thought of the living agent brings us inevitably to the thorniest question of all. What about the Ministry?

St. Luke had reached only chapter six of his second book when he recorded the decision of the Twelve that it was unreasonable for them to leave the word of God and serve tables and that they had to give their whole time to prayer and the ministry of the word. Other movements which have begun with the intention of abjuring a full time ministry have found the same sort of thing—the Salvation Army may be cited as a modern and familiar example.

A full time ministry is part of the earthly life of the Church, yet it is fraught with the greatest of dangers. It is sad enough when the full time minister begins to regard himself as essentially different from his fellow Christians. It is even sadder when his fellow Christians begin to regard themselves as essentially different from their full time minister. In other words, when the laity cheerfully assure themselves "We pay a parson. We don't have to do the work ourselves," then indeed a cell in the Body of Christ is decaying rapidly, or indeed, has already decayed.

The fact of membership both authorises and commits every Christian to continue as Christ's faithful soldier and servant to his life's end. He cannot contract out by hiring a parson to say his prayers for him or to add the tiny segment of proclamation for which he is responsible. That is not to say that there is no difference between ordained minister and laity. But it is to assert that both have identical duties, though those duties are expressed in different ways. My eyes and my feet have identical duties of contributing to the welfare of my whole being but I soon hit a lamp post if I confuse their functions.

But let nothing cloud the fact that the duty laid upon Christians is laid upon the weak and the strong, the vocal and the voiceless, the wise and the simple, the ordained and the unordained. And let nothing obscure the realisation that for the time being at least, there are simply not enough ordained men to go round.

Bishop Stephen Neill has quoted a report from *The Times* which stated that for the first time in history a Protestant minister of religion was to take up residence in Kabul, Afghanistan, one of the countries which has always been most firmly sealed off from Christian propaganda. When the new minister arrived he did not have to start from scratch but was able to take over a congregation formed ten years before on the initiative of a British Ambassador and kept in being by the efforts of lay folk.

Bishop Neill also reminds us of the impression made on continental travellers on a British ship when the Captain, treating it as part of his normal duties, reads prayers on a Sunday morning.

But are such events so rare as to be worthy of special mention? And if so, must they remain so?

There is no doubt that the Church overseas has gone much further than the Church at home in the use of laity. How many millions of Christians will rise and bless the efforts of a humble catechist? Let a European missionary speak: "Here in Rhodesia we have suffered one serious loss during the year, for an old and very dear catechist died after a short illness. He was a Fingo and was a link with the first missionaries to come here. He was known affectionately as 'Baba' or 'Father.' I stood by his grave, a little heap of earth covered with stones to protect it from the jackals out in the wide open veldt. I thought of the power of the Christ-like life in the midst of so much evil and confusion here in Africa. Such a life as his commends itself to us all. Love attracts, unites and is supreme."

Catechists have been and are being the salt of the earth. But are they not also a sign of the weakness of the Church? Why are they not ordained? Is there something wrong with the Church's formularies? Or are the Catechists insufficiently trained, and if so, why? And would the Church use Catechists if there were enough ministers?

In any case, Catechists cannot be called a genuine lay ministry—and the emphasis there is most certainly on *lay* not on *genuine*.

What is the true mark of a lay ministry? Is it the fact that it is not paid?

A recent visitor to Borneo reports: "Special reference must be made to one of the outstations called Sikuduk. After the last war bilian timber was needed for the

Kuching compound and an order was placed with a heathen village. People of Tai'i, a well known Christian village, agreed to serve as carriers and in the execution of their duties as wood-carriers did not fail to proclaim their Christian allegiance. The result was that a considerable number of the heathen decided they ought to accept the Faith. Convinced that they could not do so effectively amid the squalor and superstition of their native place they reconnoitred a new site and built an entirely new *kampong,* carving fields from the jungle. When the time was ripe they asked for a Catechist. He was appointed by the diocese. For twelve months his work was reinforced by the Rev. Peter Howes who in due course baptised all the villagers. Eventually the Bishop trekked to Sikuduk along newly sunk logs and bamboo put in by the villagers where the ground was swampy. He reached Sikuduk soon after dawn to find it apparently deserted. Then he came to a neat square of green, the grass freshly cut. Along one side stood the men and boys and on the other the girls and women with their babies, all quite silent. To the left stood a tiny church. After much handshaking in hushed silence all filed into the church and Confirmation was administered. Immediately afterwards the Bishop cele-brated the Holy Mysteries and the newly confirmed knelt at the altar rails. As the congregation filed out of the humble church the hearts of many were full to overflowing. For a few minutes conversation seemed out of place. Then the Bishop and his companions sat down to a hearty meal and then the handshaking began again. . . ."

There, surely, we see the Church in action. There, by the grace of God, all frontiers are down and no barriers divide. That lovely moment in the Borneo jungle began when Christian villagers gossiped their Faith as part of their ordinary intercourse with other villagers. It was begun by the truly lay ministry of ordinary Christians as they carried wood. But an ordained minister was fully involved and was called for by the new villagers to supplement the worthy efforts of their catechist.

Is the Church right in insisting that certain acts and ceremonies could be performed only by an ordained minister? That is another question we leave to the reader. But we do comment that if the Church is right in insisting on the offices of such then it cannot possibly be right in allowing them to be so few and far between.

But how is this paucity of ordained ministers to be overcome? Clearly they will be men who have had special training for their work, even as the scientist has for his. But equally clearly the younger Churches to a large degree lack the facilities for giving such training. They must therefore continue for some time to need the presence of "missionaries" from the older Churches.

Now in a sense we may have overdone our statements about the growth of the overseas Church. If we have built up an impression that it can get from its own ranks all the clergy it needs, how unfortunate has been our exaggeration. The younger Churches themselves keep repeating their desire for missionaries—and frequently it is the ones which have most autonomy who make the loudest requests for European help.

"Missionaries," in the good old fashioned sense of men who cross geographical frontiers to preach Christ Crucified, are still very much needed. But they must remember that the sacrifices they have made in leaving their own familiar home country do not confer upon them the stature of supermen in the eyes of the people to whom they go. When they see a missionary the people of India or Africa or Japan or elsewhere are likely to ask many questions, though innate politeness might leave those questions unspoken. Why has this man come? Does he think himself superior? Is he a spiritual aggressor? What is he expecting to get out of it? Is he in some hidden way connected with his home government? Has he come to dominate? Has he chosen to be here because there is something in his own country he would prefer to avoid? The missionary knows quite well he is there because of an act of obedience in response to a divine call, but other people are apt to attribute other motives.

The process of time which seems to conduct such a continual war of attrition upon the value of words has made "missionary" suspect. Increasingly we shall probably hear a new bit of jargon in its place—"fraternal worker." Is such a phrase just a play on words? It at least conveys a sense of brotherhood but it loses the sense of "sent." But whatever the word used, the result is going to be the same unless the man who bears it is the right sort of character. And he must remember that he goes forth not as a spiritual technician blessed with vast stores of western know-how but as a man of God "among you as he that serves." One of the best missionaries I know—and he must be nameless —is a man who seems to break every rule in the book but the Africans who know him are deeply aware that his whole being is diffused with love. And charity of that sort can cover a multitude of deficiencies as well as of sins.

Such men are still needed. And they still need to wear dog-collars, or at least their equivalent. We are not, of course, advocating a particular form of clerical dress for equatorial Africa and Labrador but just maintaining that ordained ministers are needed in both.

But that does not complete the need.

There is another delightful bit of new jargon (can it be possible that mission houses are the Church's most fertile source of technical shoptalk?) which will probably increasingly smite our ears. It must come in before this chapter can be allowed to end. It is "the non-professional missionary." This highly suggestive term has nothing to do with parsons who have, so to speak, never accepted money for their services and can therefore remain in an amateur league. It is rather concerned with those who in many ways have been the greatest hindrance to the growth of the worldwide Church.

The "non-professional missionary" is one who goes from a nominally Christian country to a nominally "mission-field" country to do some job of work. Perhaps he is to plant rubber or build bridges or sell soap powders. Perhaps he will sit in a government office or teach in some secular school. It is worth saying that there seems to be more of him about the world than ever. We are told that there are more English civilians in India now than before 1947. If we accept both English and American within the term "European" there are certainly more Europeans scattered over the world than there have ever been.

As far as many Asians and Africans are concerned, such men are the only standards by which they can judge the Christian Faith. They and their habits are assumed to be the result of a Christian civilisation. It is not necessary to add that not every such man is a worthy messenger of Christ. Whether through deliberate selfishness or through sheer ignorance, such people have frequently bred an in-eradicable hatred of all things European, not least the Faith.

This is a point where every Christian in this country from time to time gets a chance of doing something. Do you know someone overseas and do you keep in touch with him? You will have the occasional opportunity of remind-ing him that by him Christ is judged, whether he likes it or not. And before that man went overseas, did you arrange a "farewell service" in your local church, thereby reminding him that in this as in all things a Christian goes forth from the worshipping community? Did you realise that such a man, whatever his secular work, went forth as a member of your Christian family and, in the true sense of the word, represents you and your Master overseas?

One most promising development is the new Overseas Service run by Dr. Harry Holland. He has been able to secure the co-operation of government departments and business houses and many of their recruits for overseas posts go through the special course of training which he has devised and courses are being regularly run and well attended. Dr. Holland, himself a distinguished missionary, is able to tell such recruits for secular overseas service something of the work of the Church in the land to which they are going and how, by their ordinary way of life, they can help or hinder the work of that Church. It is a service which is highly appreciated by the recruits, their employers and the Church which welcomes them.

One last point belongs to this chapter. Today there are worldwide humanitarian organisations like the Red Cross and the United Nations Organisation and they owe much to Christianity. It would be silly to argue that had not the Christian Faith become so widespread there would have been no U.N.O. The blast from one atom bomb is enough to send men hurrying into huddles from which they might hope for some security. But it is surely true to say that without the worldwide influence of Christianity U.N.O. would have been a very different thing. It would not have had depending from it the clusters of organisations concerned with human welfare which are among its greatest vindications. One example (there are many) is enough—the World Health Organisation, more frequently known by its cabbalistic initials, WHO.

WHO is concerned not to fight disease, for that is a negative concept. Its job is to strive for health—everywhere. Because of its background it is able to cross many national boundaries. It is therefore able to cope with the fact that it is no good eradicating malarial mosquitos in one country if they are still breeding in some swamp just over the political border. WHO is able to tackle both the breeding ground and, so to speak the battleground, and thus able to do a complete job.

Such an organisation, in its material effects, is as Christian as a mission hospital and well deserves the attention of those who, while not wanting to be fully committed "missionaries" are nevertheless deeply aware of their Christian commitment. We believe that a Christian hand on the trigger of a mosquito spray can and will do more for humanity than any other.

To say this is merely to remind ourselves of the great and glorious opportunities presented to Christians in this turbulent twentieth century. The day when God wants servants is not over. It might be argued that it is just beginning. Today there are more exciting ways of crossing frontiers as well as more frontiers.

Let's thank God that all the work was not done before we came on the scene to be allowed to help!

CHAPTER 9

Ye are the branches

WE have surveyed the world's most exciting problem
with something of the speed with which an American
"does" Westminster Abbey. We have inevitably been super-
ficial and have forgotten that while Westminster Abbey is
a resting place for the unknown warriors and many of the
famous, its heart lies in the relationship of man to God.

What sort of a picture have we left?

Professor Albert Einstein is surely one of the great intellectual names of this century. He had no Christian axe
to grind. Read his words: "Only the Church stood
squarely across the path of Hitler's campaign for supres-
sing the truth. I never had any special interest in the
Church before but now I felt a great admiration and affec-
tion because the Church alone has had the courage and
persistence to stand for intellectual truth and moral
freedom. I am thus forced to confess that what I once
despised I now unreservedly praise."

It is not too much to say that those sentiments coming,
be it remembered, from a devout Jew are not entirely
alien to the minds of many people who are far from con-
fessing Christ crucified.

There are many people working for international organisations like U.N.O. and the Red Cross who would never
begin to say they are Christians, yet they are giving devoted
service to agencies which owe so much to the infiltration of
Christian thought across the world.

Across the world, secular governments, whether in nominally Christian countries or not, are giving increasingly attention to the provision of hospitals and schools and services for the weak and aged. The only ultimate motive for such good works is the compassion which is the heart of Christianity but so rarely appears in other religions. Even where State hospitals vie with Christian foundations it is the influence of the Christian Faith which has produced such competition for without it there would probably not have been State hospitals.

Today we do not read of the destruction of twins simply because they were born as twins, or the burning of child-widows. And India is working so hard to overcome the vestiges of the caste system. Writing with vast enthusiasm about Vinoba Bhave and the *Bhoodan* movement which aims to distribute more equitably the land of India, Hallam Tennyson says, "After centuries of meditative sloth the Sannyasis have come down from the Himalayan peaks, emerged from the forest hide-outs, stripped themselves of ashes and excrement, in order to endure the rigours of love in the all-too-human dust from which their forerunners shook themselves free. For this, Western virtue can claim its own share of credit. Two hundred years of missionary effort in spreading Christ's ideal of human service have had their effect. Western virtue has been crossed with Indian vision."

We can never be blind to the fact that some of those *Sannyasis* may be nearer to the Kingdom than some of us who indulge in mere lip service. Whether that is the case or not, so much of the credit for their social actions is to be laid at the door of the missionary effort.

Nor can we omit to notice that the majority of States which have recently acquired independence have adopted what is called the democratic way of life. Now Christianity is not tied to any political system, nor is any political system perfect. But it is clear that the idea of democracy, which basically is a belief in the equal rights of every man, can spring only from the Christian idea of man. It is when we see what tragic caricatures of democracy some of us have made in the West, even with our Christian background, that we are forced to wonder how far democracy can ever work in an Asian country which asserts a non-Christian loyalty. Nevertheless, it is clear that Christianity is having an effect even upon such political systems.

The disciples were surprised that Jesus had any dealings with a Samaritan. Perhaps we too would be surprised could we but see how far Christianity has invisibly penetrated ancient pagan systems and given them a complexion which can be conferred by God alone. It is an achievement, under God, of the missionary Church that while converts may not be obvious in large numbers in some places yet there may be far more conversions than we realise. Christianity has penetrated the life of most nations. But the end is not yet.

Added to the "underground" effect of Christian teaching on pagan States, of course, is the fact that in pretty well every country in the world God now has his outposts. Christian colonies exist in the most unlikely places. In almost every country there now exists a "younger Church." It is true that in many countries such a Church is, humanly speaking, weak both in numbers and quality. Less than one in a hundred in Formosa and Pakistan, hardly beginning in Nepal, scattered handfuls in the Middle East, are not numbers which condone complacency. And what can one say of the quality of the majority of Christians in a place like South America?

In many places numerically and spiritually weak, nevertheless there is a great dispersion of Christians throughout the world and even though figures are not available we may well believe that Christians form a larger percentage of our present day population than they did in the Mediterranean world two centuries after the death of our Lord. And, equally certainly, few colonies of today's Christians have to face more vigorous persecution than did the "not many strong and not many mighty" of the Roman Empire.

In any case, the Christian hope does not lie in this counting of heads, or even in attempts to calculate the Christian influence in secular states. The Christian hope is forever implanted in the word of God himself. We derive our encouragement as we derive our obligation from the command our Lord gave, together with the assurance that he is Lord of history. The hour when the woman is in travail may be a long one but, having reminded the disciples of that, Jesus went on with confident assurance "But I will see you again and your heart shall rejoice and in that day ye shall ask me nothing. In the world ye shall have tribulation but be of good cheer: I have overcome the world."

The Christian hope is eternal but we are not thereby justified in folding our hands and waiting God's final revelation. We are his agents whereby such a revelation shall come. And so we remind ourselves that many frontiers have been crossed but many remain. We remind ourselves that in the time of this dispensation there is no end to what we are called upon to do. We may be permitted to see tiny segments of the picture apparently reaching completion but we must also learn that as one part reaches finality so another part begins. Each end we reach is but a new beginning and the task remains unfinished. The frontiers are forever expanding.

How far are we ready and fit for the next step forward?

It is possibly true to say that there is more serious

religion practised in Britain today than there has been for quite a time. Thanks to Billy Graham and others, Christianity has become a talking point in the most unexpected places. Thanks to a more enlightened approach "prayer" is a word which has a meaning. It is interesting to note the number of secular publishers, primarily concerned with sales and profits, who are prepared to publish books of prayers and books about prayer. And isn't it worth noting that in the last hundred years Anglican Religious Orders have grown very considerably in strength, not to mention the important work like that being done by George Macleod at Iona or the Bruderhof Movement. And who can ignore the fact that the man who has attracted worldwide attention as the champion of the downtrodden Bantu —Trevor Huddleston—is a man who with vows of poverty, chastity and obedience could be described as having foresworn the world?

The life of prayer which flows ever stronger in the Church at home is reflected in the new ventures to which the Church puts its hand. The Commando Campaigns, the joint efforts of local churches in industry, the local councils of churches and ministers' fraternals which exercise a proper watchfulness over the doings of their own communities and find a common platform in expressing a Christian viewpoint about gambling and the atom bomb, about road accidents and new housing estates and all those other things which are a Christian concern. The increasing thought and experiment about the right use of lay men and women in the service of the Church is paralleled by the increasing number of people who offer themselves for ordination.

Nor is the Church at home absent from the realms of culture. The Church has always been the patron of the arts and continues to be. What of names like T. S. Eliot,

Benjamin Britten, Henry Moore—the list could be a very long one. And isn't Salvador Dali's greatest picture a religious one? Those who practise the higher expressions of reality, those who try to communicate beauty, are finding that God must be at the centre of their lives.

And surely in our day the Church has done more than it has for a long time in making a direct assault on the means of communication. The practices which have dignified themselves with the name "Public Relations" are not unknown to the Church. In fact it may be said that the Church has originated them all. It is an intriguing thought that, according to the *Encyclopaedia Britannica*, advertising in its modern form began with the Church. And the much talked of use of visual aids is but a development of the use and purpose of a medieval stained glass window. That the Church has made its inroads into the radio and television is surely evident from the hostile remarks of Mrs. Margaret Knight and her fellow secularists. And the number of local churches which don't have access to a film or filmstrip projector decreases daily.

The Church has also proved itself capable of a happy co-operation with Fleet Street and Fleet Street has proved how willingly it will co-operate. The Press can be a major ally, as the Ecumenical Press Service, Geneva, has found and used to the Church's benefit.

So here we are in a world where Christian influence has percolated widely, where there are at least outposts of Christians in many countries and we ourselves live in a country which has nearly two thousand years of Christian tradition and our own day shows itself less indifferent to the Faith than many of its predecessors.

Surely Christians have very little ground for the attitude of apology which so many of them adopt? Surely we must away with the laments that "if only we had more this, that or the other we could do so much more." God has committed us to work with the particular talent he has given us. And in our day we can rejoice that we have been set in such pleasant places.

But there is more to it than that. We still have to mention what is the most stimulating fact and perhaps the greatest weapon of twentieth century Christianity—the word which suffers from the disadvantage of being un-pronounceable to the ordinary man—ecumenicity.

The twentieth century, so far, has proved a century of paradox. On the one hand it has been a century of the crumbling of old familiar forms, not least the empires which Britain, Germany, France, Italy, Holland and even Japan had, either consciously or unconsciously, built up. The systems of western trade, of imports and exports and financial balances, the superiority of fleets of merchant ships as well as navies have all gone. On the other hand, the world has shrunk. Physical communications have made it one world, the human family has been brought into closer proximity with itself. And with this has grown up a solidarity of human material ambition—characterised in the attempts to form worldwide trades unions. The London Telephone Directory contains some interesting names— "World Commerce Corporation," "World Congress of Faiths," "World Federation of Mental Health," "World Friends," "World Jewish Congress," "World Nobility and Peerage," "World Secret Service Association," "World University Service" and many others.

This polarity of crumbling and unifying suggests fascina-ting byways in which we now have no time to pause. But it also suggests that "one world" is the inevitable trend of events, even though it is equally clear that the nearer each member of the world family draws the more he is likely to find things to squabble about. Since we live at a time when a strike of Australian dockworkers or of West Indian sugar labourers shows itself on our breakfast tables in a very short time we must become ever more and more aware of our worldwide responsibility as Christians. And against that unified responsibility it becomes clear that as Christians we no longer need seek reasons for reunion but must rather work for it or provide very strong arguments against it.

The worldwide fellowship of Christians is now the great "*fact* of our era," and as a fact it must be examined.

This coming together of long separated groups of Christians is historically unique. It is something which has been born of the missionary outreach of the Church. Its primary and eternal motive is that the glory of God shall be more fully served by the removal of all frontiers between Christians. But there is also another motive and it is endorsed by our Lord himself. He prayed for the unity of Christians "that the world might believe." Our missionary task is one of the great reasons for unity.

But it is at meetings of the World Council of Churches and its counterparts that the greatest scandal of disunion is most blatantly shown. Christians can talk together, pray together, read their Bibles together, plan social action together. But they cannot all have Holy Communion together, thus denying fellowship where fellowship must surely be highest. To record these things is not to imply that we know the answer but it is to acknowledge that they are alien to the will of the Father of the whole human family. We have actually succeeded in creating a frontier in him who broke all frontiers down.

Having glanced at these weaknesses of ecumenicity, let us record with enthusiasm the progress which has been made under its aegis. Not all the following can be attributed to the conscious deliberations of a body of people with headquarters in Geneva but they are certainly products of the atmosphere of ecumenicity which is focused there.

A degree of church unity has been accomplished in places like Canada and, most notably of course, in South India. The unity of the Japanese Kyodan, product of a wartime secular government, has now grown into a fuller fellowship of Christians. And in so many corners of the world like North India and the Gold Coast, not to mention our own discussions at home between Anglicans and Methodists and Anglicans and the Church of Scotland and others, serious steps towards visible unity are being taken.

Furthermore, these local unities are finding active expression in the extension of Christ's Kingdom. Surprisingly, the permanent aspect of the Conference of British Missionary Societies, with its headquarters at Edinburgh House, dates only from 1921. It may not be politic to point out that this book is the result of the existence of this Conference, but it is at least a symbol of a mutual approach to what are after all common problems.

The growing fellowship at home is reflected in the existence of significant interdenominational institutions overseas such as the great Christian teaching hospitals at Vellore and Ludhiana or the United Theological Colleges in places like India, Pakistan, Singapore and Africa, or the women's training colleges in India, Africa and elsewhere. It may be that the importance of such places lies not only in the students they send out but also in the experience of living together which Christians of different traditions get. And who would deny how far reaching that might be?

There are other examples of a united Christian approach. There is, for example, the Sudan United Mission, which gathers together Christians of various denominations, though usually they work in different areas of the country. Something of the vitality of this mission can be seen from its magazine *African Challenge* which makes the subject of an exciting book, *Through Ebony Eyes* by Trevor and Grace Shaw. A similar united mission is the Overseas Missionary Fellowship, formerly the China Inland Mission, which showed its flexibility in that when its workers were expelled from China they were able rapidly to be stationed in Malaya and other places.

A most interesting new development is the Ecumenical Centre at Dieppe where the Society for the Propagation of the Gospel has made over one of its former properties and now shares it with the French and Dutch Reformed Church. It is expected that this Centre will be much used by Scandinavian Lutherans and others.

But these local manifestations of unity are not all. There was the very imaginative treatment of "orphaned missions" during the war. This name was given to missionary work which prior to the war had been supported by countries which were precluded by war conditions from continuing such work. As far as possible such work was taken over by missions from other countries which were not so restricted. This arrangement has burgeoned into the present Inter-Church Aid Division of the World Council of Churches which acts on the principle that aid given from a *Church* to a *Church* is more acceptable than it can be from a missionary society. Not the least important part of the concept of Inter-Church Aid is that all members of the World Council of Churches, which includes both East and West, are expected to be, at least to some degree, both giving and receiving members, thus removing any suggestion of inferiority.

Another important development has been in "comity of missions." This means that one organisation will not go into an area where another is already working. But this is not without its problems in a mobile world. What happens when a Christian brought up in one tradition moves into an area served by another? What happens when people from Portuguese East Africa go to Johannesburg for temporary work and become Anglicans and then return home? Must the Anglican Church be there to meet them or should they be advised to become, say, Roman Catholics? Frontiers can be a puzzle as well as a challenge in this fluid twentieth century where constant movement baffles neat geographical compartments.

The World Council of Churches has its national counterparts in the various National Christian Councils—of which the British Council of Churches is one—both in East and West. It is these Councils which can most adequately approach their own national governments whenever need arises.

In the political sense at least, the time for missions from the West to eastern countries may be very short. China is one example of a country which has already established a different missionary relationship with the West. Nationalist tempers may well cause others to follow her example. The importance of world unity between Christians is vital in such a situation. But equally vital is the existence of individual National Christian Councils in the various countries. Such a feeling has contributed some part of the realisation for the need of such councils. It has been argued that it is the secular background of the younger churches which is responsible for the worldwide interest in Reunion.

But the ultimate motive for reunion lies not in the strength of the opposing forces. Christians who reunite merely because they can more ably battle with a hostile government may not have a very permanent basis for their unity. The motive for reunion lies in the will of God. No

Christian can but doubt that as long as disunity prevails the will of God is being hindered.

The growing degree of Christian unity across the world is not only a visible sign of the breaking down of long entrenched frontiers. It is also the sign that God is ever more and more preparing himself an instrument through which frontiers will be no more.

CHAPTER 10

Even so, come, Lord Jesus

IF you go by road from Gloucester to South Wales, travelling via the Forest of Dean, you will come to a hostelry bearing the legend, "The Last Hotel in England." If you go by road from South Wales to Gloucester, travelling via the Forest of Dean, you will come to the same hostelry but now you will notice another statement, "The *First* Hotel in England."

Here is something which is both first and last and your viewpoint is dictated by the direction in which you are going.

There are two quite separate viewpoints on the frontiers of this world. There is that which we can see from our purely human background. And there is God's. And it is true to say that our assessment of the frontiers is going to depend a great deal on the direction in which we are trying to go and the motives which govern our life.

Viewed with the earth-hugging eyes of humanity the frontiers are formidable. There are the physical frontiers of geography and race and any student of current affairs would assert that those frontiers become ever more impregnable as nationalisms rear their heads. Passports and visas have become the symbol of divided humanity with each sovereign country frantically trying to fortify its own little cave. There are the frontiers of the mind and these, too, must become ever more formidable as long as education is a patchy thing, available to some but denied to great masses. To the illiterate peon the world of books is a magic land into which he cannot hope to enter. He must inevitably feel cut off from its inhabitants. Then, too, there are the frontiers of the soul. So basic is religion to man created in God's image that either, when all men hold a common Faith, it becomes the world's great unifying force or, until that time, it remains our most divisive element. It is a delusion to find little difference between Buddhist saffron robes and the brown habit of a Franciscan. The striking resurgence of the mid-twentieth century "ancient religions" must make this frontier between Christianity and other faiths still wider.

Such frontiers have their own inner permutations and combinations, making the final total legion. There is the frontier posed by each new generation, to which has to be conveyed all the riches of its predecessors. There is the frontier created by moving populations where so many alien enclaves are set down in the midst of a sometimes hostile community. There are the frontiers created by changing social conditions—like the great gap which exists between Soviet and Czarist Russia or the Welfare State and Victorian England. There are the frontiers of culture which in some sense make each creative artist a lonely figure, cut off from his fellowmen.

The frontiers at which this book has merely glanced are realities. And in our generation so many of them are expanding, thus making our task of crossing them seem ever more difficult. The more that is accomplished of the Christian task the more, it seems, remains and we have learnt that a little Christianity, like a little knowledge, can be a dangerous thing. This is abundantly true of the half-converted individual who clings to a shred of the Faith and distorts the whole. It is equally true of a half-converted society.

Viewed soberly, then, the frontiers are more than discouraging. And as long as we remain on the ground they must continue to be so. But if you get high enough into the air even the Alps look like foothills. Which reminds us that there is another viewpoint on all frontiers. It is God's. And to us as his children God has given the awesome privilege of speaking on his behalf. Can we begin to find out what God's plans about frontiers may be?

At one moment in his rumbustious career Peer Gynt compares himself with an onion. He has, he says, taken off every skin which was around him and when he got down inside the last skin he found—nothing!

In this book we have been preoccupied with expanding frontiers in every realm of life and every part of the world. Like Davy Crockett we have tried to push those frontiers back or at least to peer over them. What lies beyond the final frontier? Can it be—nothing? Where is this whole process leading? What can we expect to happen? What is God's will? What is the final state to be? A heaven on earth? The whole earth caught up into heaven?

We do not know.

To acknowledge such ignorance is but to proclaim the infinity of God against our own narrow selves and to say that the shape of the end is God's affair not ours. But God has made us so that we are never satisfied with ignorance. The messenger is always more useful if he knows the purpose of his message as well as its content. So can we attempt to find out what the end of the story of God and man-in-relationship with him is like?

There are three possibilities. Either, by slow development, everyone will eventually be Christian. Or Christianity will eventually fade out. Or the Church will continue to grow while the forces of evil grow, too, until the final state is reached in some cataclysmic moment.

The first possibility is that of constant development, unbroken though perhaps slow and laborious. It is the evolution of history. Darwin's theory must be transferred to the spiritual world. Humanity is eventually perfectible. All we must do is to keep on for long enough and we'll be there.

Perhaps such a concept was more possible for those who lived in the heyday of Victoria's victorious western world. Things were going so well that Mr. Darwin's ideas seemed more widely applicable. We have since been through two bitter wars. We have since seen the deification of the lie in Germany, have smelt the stench of the gas chambers and have seen primitive passions adulated into Fascist virtues. We find it difficult to feel that humanity is perfectible. In any case the whole of history speaks against such an idea. What of the great Christian institutions like the medieval monasteries which deteriorated into caricatures? What of the inroads of Islam? What of the Borgias?

Even more important for us is that such a view does not accord with the Bible. The Son of Man will come as a thief in the night. The hope of the Christian Mission does not lie in gradual unbroken progress.

As for the second possibility, that Christianity should eventually fade away, as Christians we dismiss such an idea rapidly. But it deserves just a little more thought. If we are in danger of finally identifying Christianity with any of our human institutions which are its expressions, we are on very treacherous ground. Each of those churches has nourished holy souls. Each has much which is fair and lovely. But none is perfect. There is no reason to believe that the Church *as we know it* will be here a hundred years—or even a hundred months—from now. In fact there is almost a reason for believing that it won't be. Our Lord told us that in order to save our lives we must be prepared to lose them. Is it not possible that the Church itself is but a seed which must go into the ground and wither and die in order that a more glorious fruit may come forth? It is certainly possible though God has not told us that it is going to happen. We must turn to the third possibility.

In *Beginning From Jerusalem* (World Christian Books), Professor John Foster reminds us that at the end of each Gospel two notes are sounded—triumph and challenge. Triumph because of a work completed and challenge because of a task about to begin. Doesn't this accord closely with all we can see of the life of the Church on earth? No one can deny the growth of the Church. No one can deny that Christian civilisation is a phrase which has come to have a very full meaning even though there may be few real Christians in that civilisation. No one can deny that the Church is now more geographically widespread than it has ever been. But equally no one can deny that the powers of evil show no signs of weakening. The statistics of crime are bad enough. But even more frightening is the fact that in London and, no doubt, other parts of the United Kingdom, can be found men and women—*British* men and women—who dabble in all sorts of devilry. The sensational stories of the Black Mass and its concomitants are not entirely invented by the Sunday papers. And what of things like the international dope trade and prostitution? What of the way one race treats another in South Africa? What of the bland lies which have become the mark of international diplomacy? And what about the evil which lies hidden from the world (we hope) in our own hearts?

Quite certainly the human eye can find much confusion in the picture. But good and bad in their clearcut forms exist only in cowboy stories and thrillers. This world is the continuing arena of that involved mixture of original sin and the grace of God which is man. With the world peopled by such we expect only this bewildering picture of good and evil with both being intensified.

Let us not delude ourselves that the Church's task is, humanly speaking, nearly finished. The insistence on rights and indifference to duties, the erotic trivialities of the popular Press, the twisted morality of many novels, the casual regard for honesty evinced both at the factory bench and the manager's desk, are all signs of a world desperately needing redemption. And today these things are world-wide phenomena. Christianity has yet properly to begin its work in countries like Afghanistan and of the total human race only about a quarter even profess Christianity. Yet ours is described as a "great age of faith." It is a bewildering picture.

Yet the Bible confirms such a picture for us. We are assured that the earth shall be full of the glory of God as the waters cover the sea. We are equally assured that both wheat and tares shall grow together until the harvest and that such mixed growth somehow has the permission of the husbandman. Perhaps it is in the last book of the Bible that the picture assumes its sharpest form. Christians on earth must continue to be familiar with woe and must even expect that woe to intensify "for the devil is come down to you having great wrath because he knoweth that he hath but a short time."

"Long" and "short" are human categories. They have no meaning except in relation to each other and we can never hope to know in this life what "a short time" is. But there is one quite inescapable conclusion. It is that the present time has an ending, that somewhere history culminates in a moment which goes beyond history. We cannot be dallying dilettantes for ever.

The confident Christian hope is not based on human

statistics nor is it based on the most sanguine interpretations of contemporary events and future trends. The Christian hope is based upon the promise of God who cannot lie. It is his purpose "to gather together in one all things in Christ." That is what goes beyond all frontiers.

It has to be pointed out to all creatures who now suffer the bondage of corruption that Christ has won—has *won* —the victory and by that victory they can all be delivered into the glorious liberty of the children of God. This is the liberty through which all frontiers vanish.

The Christian is to go forth and proclaim to all men not because thereby Christianity will gradually come to be accepted across the whole earth but because, in so far as we dare to presume to read his mind, it appears that God is withholding his final moment until all men have had the chance of hearing of his beloved Son and what he did. It is when the Gospel has been preached to all men that the end cometh. No one will be sent away into everlasting punishment until he has been given the chance of knowing and accepting Christ.

Christians are called upon to live every moment as members of an already established Kingdom and by each thought, word and deed to prepare for the coming of the King. Christians are also bidden to accept and hallow all their intricate relationships with the rest of their fellowmen so that through them Christ in them might come to be known. At the beginning of time God created man-in-relationship with himself. Later he sent his only-begotten son, Jesus Christ, very God and very Man to renew that relationship. Jesus came and said "I am the Vine, ye are the branches." The vine and the branches mysteriously interdepend. That is God's definition of our status and our task.

And there are no frontiers between a vine and its

branches and between branch and branch. When Jesus said "Ye are the branches" he was proclaiming a fact he wished made universal for all men throughout all ages. And he was telling us that we are to be the agents through whom God will finally remove all frontiers.

So, by God's will as well as by his grace, it all comes back to us. We are called upon to overleap all frontiers, mental, physical and spiritual. The Dayak college student must find a unity with his village catechist in God through us, the bewildered Asian peasant, the cultured Brahmin and the deluded African witchdoctor must find their unity with their Creator through us.

Every time we drop a coin into a missionary box, unromantic though it may be, every time we pray "Thy kingdom come," every time we seek to learn yet more of our fellowmen and their needs, every time we show some act of love for our neighbour, we are breaching a frontier. The frontiers may be expanding. Quite certainly a few frightened men in an upper room on the day of Pentecost could not have begun to envisage the twentieth century frontiers which their successors would besiege. Probably the frontiers will expand much more. But "fear not, little flock, for it is your Father's good pleasure to give you the Kingdom."

When, where, how that may happen, we do not know. We only know we are *sent*. We only know that our only response must be obedience, obedience steadfastly to remain 'kings of the wild frontier.'